C Functions and Statements

NAME	DESCRIPTION	CHAPTER
printf()	Prints stuff on the screen. (Defined in stdio.h.)	4
strcpy()	Assigns a string to a variable. (Defined in string.h.)	6
scanf()	Gets stuff from the user. (Defined in stdio.h.)	8
if	Tests whether something is true. If it is, code happens.	11
else	Used with the if statement. If the test fails, other code happens.	11
while	A loop of code that repeats as long as something is true	14
do-while	A cousin of while	14
for	A loop of code that repeats a certain number of times	15
break	Terminates a loop.	16
continue	Causes a loop to jump back to the beginning.	16
switch	Lets you jump to other chunks of code, depending on a test condition.	17
default	The default choice in a switch	17
exit()	Exits the program. (Defined in stdlib.h.)	17
getchar()	Gets a single buffered character from the keyboard. (Defined in stdio.h.)	18
putchar()	Sends a single character to the screen. (Defined in stdio.h.)	18
getch()	Gets a single unbuffered character from the keyboard. (Defined in stdio.h.)	18
isalpha()	Tests whether a character is a letter. (Defined in ctype.h.)	19
isdigit()	Tests whether a character is a number. (Defined in ctype.h.)	19
isupper()	Tests whether a character is an uppercase letter. (Defined in ctype.h.)	19
islower()	Tests whether a character is a lowercase letter. (Defined in ctype.h.)	19

NAME	DESCRIPTION	CHAPTER
toupper()	Converts a letter to uppercase. (Defined in ctype.h.)	19
tolower()	Converts a letter to lowercase. (Defined in ctype.h.)	19
strcat()	Concatenates two strings. (Defined in string.h.)	19
gets()	Gets a string from the keyboard. (Defined in string.h.)	19
puts()	Puts a string on the screen. (Defined in string.h.)	19
floor()	Rounds a float down to the nearest integer. (Defined in math.h.)	20
ceil()	Rounds a float up to the nearest integer. (Defined in math.h.)	20
fabs()	Returns the absolute value. (Defined in math.h.)	20
pow()	Raises a value to a power. (Defined in math.h.)	20
sqrt()	Returns the square root. (Defined in math.h.)	20
rand()	Returns a random number. (Defined in stdlib.h.)	20
srand()	Seeds the rand() function. (Defined in stdlib.h.)	20
fopen()	Opens a file. (Defined in stdio.h.)	26
fclose()	Closes a file. (Defined in stdio.h.)	26
fprintf()	Prints stuff to a file. (Defined in stdio.h.)	26
fgets()	Gets strings from a file. (Defined in stdio.h.)	26
feof()	Checks for the end of a file. (Defined in stdio.h.)	26
fseek()	Goes to a specific part of a file. (Defined in stdio.h.)	27
fputc()	Puts a character in a file. (Defined in stdio.h.)	27
fgetc()	Gets a character from a file. (Defined in stdio.h.)	27
return	Returns a value from a function.	30

For more information just flip the card

Compound Assignment Operators

COMPOUND OPERATOR	EXAMPLE	EQUIVALENT STATEMENT
*=	total *= 1.25;	total = total * 1.25;
/=	amt /= factor;	amt = amt / factor;
%=	days %= 3;	days = days % 3;
+=	count += 1;	count = count + 1;
-=	adjust -= 0.5;	adjust = adjust - 0.5;

Order of Operators

LEVEL	OPERATOR	ASSOCIATIVITY
1	( ) (parentheses), [ ] (array element), . (structure member reference)	Left to right
2	- (negative sign), ++ (increment), - - (decrement), & (address-of), * (pointer indirection), sizeof( ), ! (the not operator)	Right to left
3	* (multiplication), / (division), % (modulus)	Left to right
4	+ (addition), - (subtraction)	Left to right
5	< (less than), <= (less than or equal to), > (greater than), >= (greater than or equal to)	Left to right
6	== (equal to), != (not equal to)	Left to right
7	&& (logical and)	Left to right
8	¦¦ (logical or)	Left to right
9	? : (the conditional operator)	Right to left
10	=, *=, /=, %=, +=, -= (assignment operators)	Right to left
11	, (the comma operator)	Left to right

The Basic fopen( ) Mode Strings

MODE	DESCRIPTION
"w"	Write mode that creates a new file whether it exists or not.
"r"	Read mode that lets you read an existing file. If the file doesn't exist, you get an error.
"a"	Append mode that lets you add to the end of a file or create the file if it doesn't exist.

The Random-Access fopen( ) Modes

MODE	DESCRIPTION
"r+"	Opens an existing file for both reading and writing.
"w+"	Opens a new file for writing and reading.
"a+"	Opens a file in append mode (the file pointer points to the end of the file) but lets you move back in the file, reading and writing as you go.

Conversion Characters

CONVERSION CHARACTER	DESCRIPTION
%d	Integer
%f	Floating-point
%c	Character
%s	String

Escape Sequences

CODE	DESCRIPTION
\n	Newline
\a	Alarm (the computer's bell)
\t	Tab
\\	Backslash
\"	Quotation mark

The Logical Operators

LOGICAL OPERATOR	MEANING
&&	And
¦¦	Or
!	Not

The Relational Operators

RELATIONAL OPERATOR	DESCRIPTION
==	Equal to
>	Greater than
<	Less than
>=	Greater than or equal to
<=	Less than or equal to
!=	Not equal to

The Pointer Operators

OPERATOR	DESCRIPTION
&	Address-of operator
*	Dereferencing operator

Absolute Beginner's Guide to C

Absolute Beginner's Guide to C

Greg Perry

SAMS
PUBLISHING

A Division of Prentice Hall Computer Publishing
11711 North College, Carmel, Indiana 46032 USA

*For my friend
James Nickles:
Your brother Don might
get all the publicity,
but you'll always have
my business!*

Copyright © 1993 by Sams Publishing

International Standard Book Number: 0-672-30341-8

Library of Congress Catalog Card Number: 93-83472

96 95 94 93   4 3 2 1

Interpretation of the printing code: The rightmost double-digit number is the year of the book's printing; the rightmost single-digit is the number of the book's printing. For example, a printing code of 93-1 shows that the first printing of the book occurred in 1993.

Composed in Palatino, DomCasual, and MCPdigital by Prentice Hall Computer Publishing

Printed in the United States of America

Trademarks

Overview

Contents

Part IV   C Programs and Lots of Data

Acknowledgments

My thanks go to all my friends at Sams Publishing. Most writers would refer to them as *editors;* to me they are *friends.* The acquisitions editor for the majority of my books, Stacy Hiquet, specializes in kindness and patience. (With a Kappa Sig for a husband, she'd have to, as my wife would attest!) Gayle Johnson majors in turning my questionable work into award-winning copy, and I thank her greatly. It might seem as if my writing keeps improving, but in reality, it's Gayle's editing. The dynamic duo, Keith Davenport and Dean Miller, have developed this manuscript into something for everyone, and they managed to maintain accuracy where I failed miserably. Last but not least, Richard Swadley, the big chief who gives all the grief, deserves the final credit for the success of every book from Sams. Richard's initial direction for every book seems to hit the bull's-eye, and he knows exactly what the audience needs and wants.

I want all my readers to understand this: The people at Sams Publishing care about you most of all. The things they do result from their concern for your knowledge and enjoyment.

On a more personal note, my beautiful bride Jayne, my proud parents Glen and Bettye Perry, and my friends, who wonder how I find the time to write, all deserve credit for supporting my need to write.

About the Author

Greg Perry is a speaker and writer in both the programming and applications sides of computing. He is known for bringing programming topics down to the beginner's level. Perry has been a programmer and trainer for the past 15 years. He received his first degree in computer science, and then he received a master's degree in corporate finance. Besides writing, he teaches, consults, and lectures across the country, including at the acclaimed Software Development programming conferences. Perry is the author of 17 other computer books, including *Absolute Beginner's Guide to Programming, Turbo C++ Programming 101, Moving from C to C++,* and *QBasic Programming 101* (all published by Sams Publishing). In addition, he has published articles in several publications such as *PC World, Data Training,* and *Inside First Publisher.* In his spare time, he gives lectures on traveling in Italy, his second-favorite place to be.

Introduction

Are you tired of seeing your friends get C programming jobs while you're left out in the cold? Would you like to learn C but just don't have the energy? Is your old, worn-out computer in need of a hot programming language to spice up its circuits? This book is just what the doctor ordered!

Absolute Beginner's Guide to C breaks the commonality of computer books by talking to you at your level without talking down to you. This book is like your best friend sitting next to you teaching C. *Absolute Beginner's Guide to C* attempts to *express* without *impressing*. It talks to you in plain language, not in "computerese." The short chapters, line drawings, and occasionally humorous straight talk guide you through the maze of C programming faster, friendlier, and easier than any other book available today.

Who's This Book For?

This is a beginner's book. If you have never programmed before, this book is for you. No knowledge of any programming concept is assumed. If you can't spell C, you can learn to program in C with this book.

The phrase *absolute beginner* has different meanings at different times. Maybe you've tried to learn C before but gave up. Many books and classes make C much more technical than it is. You might have programmed in other languages but are a beginner in C. If so, read on, o faithful one, because in 30 quick chapters, you'll know C.

What Makes This Book Different?

This book doesn't cloud issues with internal technical stuff that beginners in C don't need. The author (me) is of the firm belief that introductory principles have to be taught well and slowly. Once you tackle the basics, the "harder" parts never seem hard. This book teaches you the real C that you need to get started.

C can be an extremely cryptic and difficult language. Many people try to learn C more than once. The problem is simply this: Any subject, whether it be brain surgery, mail sorting, or C programming, is easy if it's explained properly. Nobody can teach you anything, because you have to teach yourself, but if the instructor, book, or video doing the teaching doesn't make the subject simple and *fun*, you won't *want* to learn the subject.

I challenge you to find a more straightforward approach to C than is offered in *Absolute Beginner's Guide to C*. If you can, call me because I'd like to read it. (You thought maybe I'd offer you your money back?) Seriously, I've tried to provide you with a different kind of help from that which you find in most other places.

The biggest advantage that this book offers is that the author (still me) really *likes* to write C programs and likes to teach C even more. I believe that you will learn to like C, too.

This Book's Design Elements

Like many computer books, this book contains lots of helpful hints, tips, warnings, and so on. You will run across many *icons* (little pictures) that bring these specific items to your attention. A glance at the icon gives you an idea of the purpose of the text next to the icon. Here are descriptions of this book's icons:

YIKES!

This icon points out potential problems you could face with the particular topic being discussed. Often the icon indicates a warning you should heed, or it provides a way to fix a problem that can occur.

PSST! Many of this book's hints and tips (and there are lots of them) are highlighted by this icon. When a really neat feature or code trick coincides with the topic you're reading about, this icon pinpoints just what you can do to take advantage of the added bonus.

HMM... Throughout the C language, certain subjects provide a deeper level of understanding than others. This icon tells you about something you might not have thought about before, such as a new use for the topic being discussed.

Skip This, It's Technical

If you don't want anything more than the beginning essentials of C, don't read the material next to this icon. Actually, you probably will enjoy this material, but you can safely skip it without losing your understanding of the chapter.

Occasionally you will see a **Fun Fact** in the margin. These Fun Facts convey interesting information about computers, programming, and the C language.

Each chapter ends by reviewing the key points you should remember from that chapter. The items under the **Happy Landings** and **Shot Down** headings list things you should and shouldn't do. One of the key features that ties everything together is the **In Review** section. This chapter summary states the chapter's primary goal, lists a code example that highlights the concepts taught, and provides a code analysis that offers an explanation of that code example. You'll find these chapter summaries, which begin in Chapter 2, to be a welcome wrap-up of the chapter's main points.

This book uses the following typographic conventions:

- Code lines, variables, and any text you see on-screen appears in monospace.

- Placeholders on format lines appear in *italic monospace*.

- Parts of program output that the user typed appear in **bold monospace**.

- New terms appear in *italic*.

- Optional parameters in syntax explanations are enclosed in flat brackets ([ ]). You do *not* type the brackets when you include these parameters.

How Can I Have Fun with C?

Appendix B contains a complete, working Blackjack program. The program was kept as short as possible without sacrificing readable code and game-playing functionality. The game also had to be kept generic in order to work on all C compilers. Therefore, you won't find fancy graphics, but once you learn C, you'll easily be able to access your compiler's specific graphics, sound, and data-entry routines to improve the program.

The program uses as much of this book's contents as possible. Almost every topic taught in this book appears in the Blackjack game. Too many books offer nothing more than snippets of code. The Blackjack game gives you the chance to see the "big picture." As you progress through this book, you'll understand more and more of the game.

What Do I Do Now?

Turn the page and learn the C language.

Part 1
First Steps with C

Never underestimate the importance of
protective eyewear and computer programming!

What Is C Programming?

Rewarding and Fun

Fun Fact
C evolved from a computer language named B. Both were developed at Bell Labs.

Although some people consider C to be difficult to learn and use, they're wrong. C is touted as being a cryptic programming language, and it can be, but a well-written C program is just as easy to follow as a program written in any other programming language. The demand for C programmers today is high, and there is no end in sight to that demand.

In case you've never written a program in your life, this chapter begins at the beginning, teaching you introductory programming concepts, explaining what a program is, and providing a short history of the C language. Get ready to be excited! C is a programming language rich in capabilities.

What Is a Program?

A computer isn't smart. On your worst days, you are light-years ahead of your computer in intelligence. The computer's only advantage is that it obeys your instructions. Your computer will sit for days, processing the data you supply, without getting bored and without wanting overtime pay.

The computer can't decide what to do on its own. Because computers can't think for themselves, they must be given extremely detailed instructions. Without instructions, a computer is useless. A computer can no more process your payroll without detailed instructions than an automobile can start by itself and drive around the block. The detailed instructions you supply when you want your computer to perform a specific task are known as a *program.*

HMM...

Word processors, computer payroll systems, computer games, and electronic spreadsheets are nothing more than computer programs. Without such programs, the computer would just sit there, not knowing what to do next. A word processing program contains a list of detailed instructions, written in a computer language such as C, that tells the computer exactly how to be a word processor. When you *run* a program, you are telling the computer to follow the instructions in the program you have supplied.

There are thousands of programs you can buy for your computer, but when a business wants a computer to perform a specific task, it hires programmers to write programs that follow the specifications needed by the business. You can make your computer do many things, but you might not be able to find a program that does exactly what you want. This book rescues you from that dilemma. After you learn C, you will be able to write programs that contain instructions that tell the computer how to behave.

PSST! A computer program tells your computer how to do what you want. Just as a chef needs a recipe to make a dish, a program needs instructions to produce results. (See Figure 1.1.) A recipe is nothing more than a set of detailed instructions that, if properly written, describes the proper sequence and contents of the steps needed to prepare a certain dish. That's exactly what a computer program is to your computer.

Programs produce *output* when you *run* or *execute* them. The prepared dish is a recipe's output, and the payroll or word processor is the output produced by a running program.

Figure 1.1.

Just as a chef needs a recipe to cook, your computer needs a program to know what to do next.

What You Need to Write C Programs

Before you can write and execute a C program on your computer, you need a *C compiler*. A C compiler takes the C program you write and *compiles* it (which is a technical term for making the program computer-readable), enabling you to run the compiled program when you're ready to look at the results. Today's C compilers are much more advanced than the language compilers of a few years ago. They offer full-screen editing, pull-down menus, and online help to provide more assistance to the beginning programmer.

An advanced version of C, known as C++, is sold with almost every C compiler. Therefore, when you shop for a C compiler, you will almost always find a C and a C++ compiler combined in the same box. Buy the combined package so that you will have C now and C++ when you're ready to learn it.

The most popular C compiler in use today is *Turbo C++*, made by Borland International, Inc. Borland also offers *Borland C++*, which is Turbo C++ along with many additional programs that help advanced C and C++ programmers. All the popular C++ compilers, including Borland's, are both C and C++ compilers.

Microsoft Corporation also offers two versions of C. Its *QuickC* compiler is an easy-to-use compiler that is great for beginning C programmers. Microsoft also offers a C++ compiler, the *Visual C++ compiler*, for large-scale programming applications.

There are other C compiler vendors on the market, but Borland and Microsoft lead the pack in sheer numbers of C programming customers.

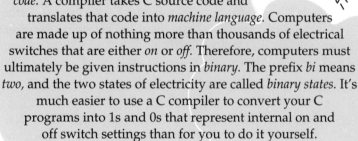

Skip This, It's Technical

The C program you write is called *source code.* A compiler takes C source code and translates that code into *machine language.* Computers are made up of nothing more than thousands of electrical switches that are either *on* or *off.* Therefore, computers must ultimately be given instructions in *binary.* The prefix *bi* means *two,* and the two states of electricity are called *binary states.* It's much easier to use a C compiler to convert your C programs into 1s and 0s that represent internal on and off switch settings than for you to do it yourself.

The Programming Process

Most people follow these basic steps when writing a program:

1. Decide exactly what the program is to do.

2. Use an *editor* to write and save your programming language instructions. An editor is a lot like a word processor (although not usually as fancy) that lets you create and edit text. All the popular C compilers include an integrated editor along with the programming language compiler. All C program filenames end in .C.

3. Compile the program.

4. Check for program errors. If there are any, fix them and go back to step 3.

5. Execute the program.

An error in a computer program is called a *bug*. Getting rid of errors is called *debugging* a program.

Today's C compilers, such as Turbo C and QuickC, let you perform these five steps easily, all from within the same environment. For instance, if you have Turbo C or QuickC, you can use Turbo C's editor, compile your program, view any errors, fix the errors, run the program, and look at the results, all from within the same screen and using a uniform set of menus.

YIKES!

If you have never programmed before, this all might seem confusing. Relax. Most of today's C compilers come with a handy tutorial you can use to learn the basics of the compiler.

In a nutshell, most C compilers require only this of you when you write C programs: Start the compiler, type your program, then press Alt-R (press and hold the Alt key, press the R key, then let up on both) to run your program. The compiler takes care of compiling and executing the program.

PSST!   Many times, your C compiler can find bugs in your programs. If you spell a command incorrectly, for instance, your C compiler tells you so when you compile the program.

Using C

C is one of the most popular programming languages in use today. Because of the many possible versions of C, a committee known as the *ANSI* committee (*American National Standards Institute*) developed a set of rules (known as *ANSI C*) for all versions of C. As long as you run programs using an ANSI C compiler, you can be assured that you can compile your C programs on almost any computer that has an ANSI C compiler. By choosing the appropriate setting, you can make most compilers, including Borland's and Microsoft's, ANSI C compatible. (See your compiler manual for details.)

Fun Fact
In 1983, ANSI created the X3J11 committee to set a standard version of C. This became known as ANSI C.

PSST! As soon as you compile a C program, you can run the compiled program on any computer that is compatible with yours, whether or not the computer has an ANSI C compiler.

C is more efficient than most programming languages. It is also a relatively small programming language. In other words, you don't have to learn many *commands* in C. Throughout this book, you will learn about C commands and other elements of the C language, such as operators, functions, and preprocessor directives.

YIKES!
Put on your thinking cap and set your phaser on C, because the next chapter takes you on a journey through your first C program.

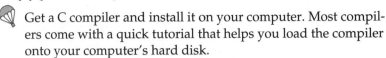

Happy Landings

 Get a C compiler and install it on your computer. Most compilers come with a quick tutorial that helps you load the compiler onto your computer's hard disk.

Learn the C programming language. This book takes care of that! As you learn more about C, try to stay with ANSI C commands instead of using compiler-specific C functions that might not be available in other compilers you use later.

Shot Down

Don't be nervous, because C programs can be easy to write. C compilers often have many more features than you will ever have to learn.

How Do I Get Started in C?

With the main() Function

You get to see your first C program in this chapter! Please don't try to understand *every* character of the C programs discussed here. Relax and just get familiar with the look and feel of C. After a while you will begin to recognize elements common to all C programs.

Getting a Glimpse

This section shows you a short but complete C program and discusses another that appears in Appendix B. Both programs contain common and different elements. The first program is extremely simple. Here it is:

```c
/* Prints a message on the screen */
#include <stdio.h>
main()
{
   printf("This C stuff is easy!\n");
   return 0;
}
```

If you were to type this program using your C compiler's editor, compile the program, and run it, you would see this message appear on the screen:

```
This C stuff is easy!
```

YIKES!

It took a lot of work to produce that one-line message! Actually, of the seven lines in the program, only one—the one that starts with `printf`—does the work that produces the output. The other lines provide "housekeeping chores" common to most C programs.

PSST! To see a really long program, glance at Appendix B. Although the Blackjack game there spans several pages, it too contains elements common to the shorter program you just saw.

Look through both the programs just discussed and notice any similarities. One of the first things you might notice is the use of braces, {}, parentheses, (), and backslashes, \. Be careful when typing C programs into your C compiler. C gets picky if you accidentally type a square bracket, [, when you should type a brace, {, and so on.

HMM... C isn't picky about everything. For instance, most of the spacing you see in C programs serves to make the programs clearer to people, not to C. As you program, add blank lines and indent sections of code that go together to help the appearance of the program and to make it easier for you to find what you are looking for.

PSST! Use the Tab key to indent instead of typing a bunch of spaces.

C requires that you use lowerase letters for all commands and predefined functions. (You'll learn what a function is in the next section.) About the only time you use uppercase letters is on a line with #define and inside the printed messages you write.

The main() Function

The most important part of a C program is its main() function. Both of the programs discussed earlier have main() functions. Although at this point the distinction is not critical, main() is a C *function*, not a C command. A function is a routine that comes with C or that you write. A function is nothing more than a routine that performs some task. C programs are made up of one or more functions. Each program must *always* include a main() function. A function is distinguished from a command by the parentheses that follow the function name. These are functions:

```
main()    calcIt()    printf()    strlen()
```

and these are commands:

```
return    while    int    if    float
```

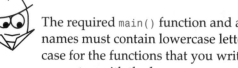

YIKES!

One of the functions just listed, calcIt(), contains an uppercase letter. However, the preceding section said you should stay away from uppercase. If a name has multiple parts, such as doReportPrint(), it's common practice to use uppercase letters to begin some of the words to increase readability. (Spaces aren't allowed in function names.) Stay away from typing words in *all* uppercase. An uppercase letter for clarity is okay.

PSST!   The required main() function and all of C's supplied function names must contain lowercase letters. You can use uppercase for the functions that you write, but most C programmers stay with the lowercase convention.

main() is always the first place the computer begins when running your program. If main() is not the first function listed in your program, main() still marks the beginning of the program's execution. Therefore, you should make main() the first function in every program you write. The programs in the next several chapters have only one main() function.

After the word main(), you always see an opening brace, {. When you find a matching closing brace, }, main() is finished. There might be pairs of braces within a main() function as well. For practice, look again at the long program in Appendix B. main() is the first function with code, and several other functions follow, each with braces and code.

The statement #include <stdio.h> is needed in almost every C program. It helps with printing and getting data. For the time being, always put this statement somewhere before main(). You will understand it later.

Kinds of Data

Your C programs must use data made up of numbers, words, and characters, and they process that data into meaningful information. Although there are many different kinds of data, the following three data types are by far the most common used in C programming:

 Characters

 Integers

 Floating-points (also called *real numbers*)

YIKES!

"How much math am I going to have to learn?! I didn't think that was part of the bargain!" you yell. Well, you can relax, because C does your math for you; you don't have to be able to add 2 and 2 to write C programs. You do, however, have to understand data types so that you will know how to choose the correct type when you need it.

Fun Fact
The American National Standards Institute (ANSI), which developed ANSI C, also developed the code for the ASCII chart.

C's Characters

A C *character* is any single character your computer can represent. Your computer knows 256 different characters. Each of them is found in something called the *ASCII table,* located in your compiler's manual. (ASCII is pronounced *ask-ee*. If you don't *know-ee,* you can just *ask-ee.*) Anything your computer can represent can be a character. Any or all of the following can be considered characters:

```
A     a     4     %     Q     !     +     =     ]
```

PSST! Even the Spacebar produces a character. C has to keep track of any blanks your program needs, just as it needs to keep track of the letters of the alphabet and the other characters.

As you can see, every letter, number, and space is a character to C. Sure, a 4 looks like a number, and it sometimes is, but it is also a character. If you want 4 to be a character, you can't do math with it. If you want 4 to be a number, you can do math with it. The same holds for the special symbols. The plus sign is a character, but the plus sign also performs addition. (There I go, bringing math back into the conversation!)

All of C's character data is enclosed in *apostrophes* (`'`). Some people call apostrophes *single quotation marks*. Apostrophes differentiate character data from other kinds of data, such as numbers and math symbols. For example, in a C program, all of the following are character data:

```
'A'      'a'      '4'      '%'      ' '      '-'
```

None of the following can be character data because they have no apostrophes around them:

```
A      a      4      %      -
```

PSST!   None of the following are valid characters. Only single characters, not multiple characters, can go inside apostrophes.

```
'C is fun'  'C is hard'  'I should be sailing instead
of this.'
```

The first program in this chapter contains the character `'\n'`. At first, you might not think `\n` is a single character, but it's one of the few two-character combinations that C interprets as a character. This will make more sense later.

If you need to specify more than one character (except for the special characters that you'll learn, like the `\n` just described), enclose the characters in *quotation marks*, `" "`. Multiple characters are called *strings*. The following is a C string:

```
"C is fun to learn."
```

HMM... That's really all you need to know about characters and strings for now. Later in this book you'll learn how to use them in programs. When you see how to store characters in variables, you'll see why the apostrophe and quotation marks are important.

Numbers in C

Although you might not have thought about it before now, numbers take on many different sizes and shapes. Your C program must have a way to store numbers, no matter what the numbers look like. You must store numbers in numeric variables. Before you look at variables, a review of the kinds of numbers will help.

Whole numbers are called *integers.* Integers have no decimal points. (Remember this rule: Like most members of Congress, integers have no point whatsoever.) Any number without a decimal point is an integer. All of the following are integers:

```
10    54    0    -121    -68    752
```

Skip This, It's Technical

Never begin an integer with a leading 0 (unless the number *is* zero), or C will think you typed the number in *hexadecimal* or *octal*. Hexadecimal and octal, sometimes called *base-16* and *base-8*, respectively, are weird ways of representing numbers. 053 is an octal number, and 0x45 is a hexadecimal number. If you don't know what all that means, just remember for now that C puts a *hex* on you if you mess around with leading zeroes before integers.

Numbers with decimal points are called *floating-point numbers.* All of the following are floating-point numbers:

```
547.43      0.0      0.44384      9.1923      -168.470      .22
```

PSST! As you can see, leading zeroes are okay in front of floating-point numbers.

The choice of using integers or floating-point numbers depends on the data your programs are working with. Some values (such as ages and quantities) make great integers, while other values (such as money amounts) make great floating-point numbers. Internally, C stores integers differently from floating-point values, however. As you can see from Figure 2.1, a floating-point value usually takes twice as much memory as an integer. Therefore, if you can get away with using integers, do so and save floating-points for values that need the decimal point.

Figure 2.1.

It often takes more memory to store floating-point values than integers.

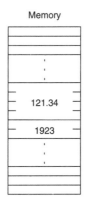
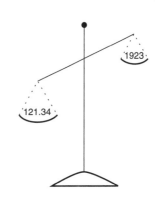

Figure 2.1 shows you that integers generally take less memory than floating-point values, no matter how large or small the values stored there are. On any given day, a large post office box might get much less mail than a smaller one. The contents of the box don't affect what the box happens to hold. The size of C's number storage is affected not by the value of the number, but by the type of the number.

Different C compilers use different amounts of storage for integers and floating-point values. As you will learn later, there are ways of finding out exactly how much memory your C compiler uses for each type of data.

Happy Landings

Keep the Caps Lock key off! Most C commands and functions require lowercase letters.

Put lots of extra spacing in your C programs to make them more readable.

A C function must have parentheses following its name. A C program consists of one or more functions. The `main()` function is always required. C executes `main()` before any other function.

If you use a character, enclose it in single quotes. Strings go inside quotation marks. Integers are whole numbers without decimal points. Floating-point numbers have decimal points.

Shot Down

Don't be sloppy about your typing. When C needs a certain special character such as a brace, a square bracket will not do.

Don't put leading zeroes before integers unless the integer *is* zero.

In Review

This chapter's goal was to familiarize you with the "look and feel" of a C program, primarily the `main()` function that includes executable C statements. As you saw, C is a free-form language that isn't picky about spacing. C is, however, picky about lowercase letters. C requires lowercase spellings of all its commands and functions, such as `printf()`.

At this point, don't worry about the specifics of the code you see in this chapter. The rest of the book explains all the details.

Code Example

```
/* Prints a character and some numbers */
#include <stdio.h>
main()
{
   printf("A letter grade of %c\n", 'B');
   printf("A test score of %d\n", 87);
   printf("A class average of %.1f\n", 85.9);
   return 0;
}
```

Code Analysis

This short program does nothing more than print three messages on the screen. Each message includes one of the three data types mentioned in this chapter.

The `main()` function is the only function in the program written by the programmer. The left and right braces, { and }, always enclose `main()`'s code as well as any other function's code that you might add to your programs. The other function, `printf()`, is a built-in C function that produces output. Here is the program's output:

```
A letter grade of B
A test score of 87
A class average of 85.9
```

How Do I Know What's Happening?

Through Comments

Your computer must be able to understand your programs. Because the computer is a dumb machine, you must be careful to spell C commands exactly right and type them in the same order you want them executed. However, people also read your programs. You will change your programs often, and if you write programs for a company, the company's needs will change over time. You must ensure that your programs are understandable to people as well as to computers. Therefore, you should document your programs by explaining what they do.

Commenting on Your Code

Throughout a C program, you should add *comments.* Comments are messages scattered throughout your programs that explain what's going on. If you write a program to calculate payroll, the program's comments explain the gross pay calculations, state tax calculations, federal tax calculations, social security calculations, and all the other calculations that are going on.

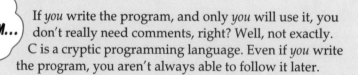

If *you* write the program, and only *you* will use it, you don't really need comments, right? Well, not exactly. C is a cryptic programming language. Even if *you* write the program, you aren't always able to follow it later.

PSST! Add comments as you write your programs. Get in the habit now, because programmers rarely go back and add comments later. When they must make a change later, programmers often lament about their program's lack of comments.

Comments are *not* C commands. C ignores every comment in your program. Comments are for people, and the programming statements residing between the comments are for the computer. (See Figure 3.1.)

Figure 3.1.

Comments are for people, and C programming statements are for the computer.

There's another reason you should comment. As you write a program, you often have to glance through the code you've written. Reading through comments instead of C programming statements is much quicker. If you didn't comment, you'd have to decipher your C code every time you looked through a piece of it.

Consider the following C statement:

```
return ((s1 < s2) ? s1 : s2;
```

You don't yet know C, but even if you did, this statement takes some study to figure out. Isn't this better:

```
return ((s1 < s2) ? s1 : s2; /* Gets the smaller of 2 values */
```

The next section explains the syntax of comments, but for now, you can see that the message between the /* and the */ is a comment.

The closer a comment is to spoken language, and the further a comment is from C code, the better the comment is. Don't write a comment just for the sake of commenting. The following statement's comment is useless:

```
printf("Payroll");  /* Prints the word "Payroll" */
```

YIKES!

You don't yet know C and you *still* don't need the preceding line's comment! Redundant comments are a waste of your time and don't add anything to programs. Add comments to explain what is going on to people (including yourself) who might need to read your program.

Specifying Comments

C comments begin with /* and end with */. Comments can span several lines in a program, and they can go just about anywhere in a program. All of the following lines contain C comments:

```
/* This is a comment that happens to span two lines
   before coming to an end */

/* This is a single-line comment */

for (i = 0; i < 25; i++)  /* Counts from 0 to 25 */
```

HMM... Notice that comments can go on lines by themselves or before or after programming statements. The choice of placement depends on the length of the comment and the amount of code the comment describes.

The Blackjack program in Appendix B contains all kinds of comments. By reading through the comments in that program, you can get an idea of what the program does without ever looking at the C code itself.

Don't comment every line. Usually only every few lines need comments. Many programmers like to place a multiline comment before a section of code and then insert a few smaller comments on lines that need them. Here is a complete program with different kinds of comments:

```c
/* Filename: AVG.C */
/* Computes the average of three class grades */
#include <stdio.h>
main()
{
   float gr1, gr2, gr3;  /* Variables to hold grades */
   float avg;            /* Variable to hold average */
   /* Asks for each student's grade */
   printf("What grade did the first student get? ");
   scanf(" %f", &gr1);
   printf("What grade did the second student get? ");
   scanf(" %f", &gr2);
   printf("What grade did the third student get? ");
   scanf(" %f", &gr3);

   avg = (gr1 + gr2 + gr3) / 3.0;  /* Computes average */
   printf("\nThe student average is %.2f", avg);
   return 0;  /* Goes back to DOS */
}
```

Many companies require that their programmers embed their own names in comments at the top of programs they write. If changes need to be made to the program later, the original programmer can be found to help out. It's also a good idea to include the filename that you use to save the program on disk at the beginning of a program so that you can find a program on disk when you run across a printed listing.

This book might overcomment in some places. You are so unfamiliar with C that every little bit of explanation helps.

Skip This, It's Technical

For testing purposes, you might find it useful to *comment out* a section of code by putting a /* and */ around it. By doing this, you cause C to ignore that section of code, and you can concentrate on the piece of code you're working on. Do not, however, comment out a section of code that already contains comments, because you cannot embed one comment within another. The first */ that C runs across triggers the end of the comment you started. When C finds the next */ without a beginning /*, you get an error.

The Future of Comments

Many of today's C compilers support another kind of comment that was originally developed for C++ programs. This new kind of comment is not approved for use by ANSI C, but might be someday soon because it's so popular. The new style of comment begins with two slashes, //, and ends only at the end of the line.

Here is a sample of the new style of comment:

```
// Short program!
#include <stdio.h>
main()
{
   printf("Looking good!");  // A message
   return 0;
}
```

Because the new style of comment isn't sanctioned by the ANSI C committee, this book doesn't use it again. However, you should become familiar with this style because it's easier to use than /* and */, and many C programmers are beginning to use it.

Happy Landings

 The three rules of programming are comment, comment, comment. Use comments abundantly.

 When you want to comment, begin with /*. End the comment with */.

 If you want to use the new style of comment, begin the comment with //. This kind of comment, however, isn't yet approved by ANSI C.

Shot Down

 Don't use redundant comments. Worthless comments aren't helpful, and they waste valuable programming time.

 Don't nest one comment inside another. If you want to comment out a section of your program, you must make sure that the section doesn't contain other comments.

In Review

You must add comments to your programs, not for computers, but for people. Although C programs can be cryptic, comments eliminate lots of confusion. A comment is just a message that describes what's going on in the C code.

Anything between the /* and */ is a C comment. C ignores all comments because it knows that comments are for people.

Code Example

Here are two lines without comments:

```
scanf(" %d", &a);
yrs = (a >= 21) ? 0 : 21 - a;
```

Here are the same two lines with comments:

```
scanf(" %d", &a);  /* Gets the user's age */
yrs = (a >= 21) ? 0 : 21 - a;  /* Calculates the number of
                                  years until adulthood */
```

Code Analysis

As you can see from these lines, it's not always obvious what goes on in C programs. Comments explain in plain spoken language exactly what's going on with the code. Not every line in every C program needs a comment, but many do to clarify what's happening.

4

Can I See Results?

With printf()

If neither you nor anybody else could see your program's output, there would be little use for your program! Ultimately, you have to be able to view the results of a program. C's primary means for output is the `printf()` function. There is no actual command that performs output, but the `printf()` function is a part of every C compiler and one of the most-used features of the language.

What printf() Does

In a nutshell, `printf()` produces output on your screen. As Figure 4.1 shows, `printf()` sends characters, numbers, and words to the screen. There is a lot to `printf()`, but you don't have to be an expert in all the `printf()` options (very few C programmers are) to use `printf()` for all your program's screen output.

Figure 4.1.

printf() sends characters, numbers, and words to the screen.

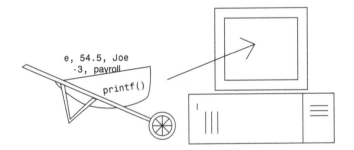

The Format of printf()

`printf()` takes many forms, but once you get used to its format, `printf()` is easy to use. Here is the general format of `printf()`:

```
printf(controlString [, data]);
```

Skip This, It's Technical

`printf()` doesn't actually send output to your screen, but to your computer's *standard output device.* Most operating systems, including MS-DOS, route the standard output to your screen unless you know enough about MS-DOS to route the output elsewhere. Most of the time you can ignore this standard output device stuff because you'll almost always want output to go to the screen. Other C functions you will learn about later route output to your printer and disk drives.

YIKES!

This book often shows the *format* of commands and functions when you first see them. The format is the general look of the statement. If something in a format appears in brackets, such as , *data* just shown, that part of the statement is optional. You almost never type the brackets themselves. If brackets are required in the command, that is made clear in the text following the format. `printf()` requires a *controlString*, but not *data* following it.

YIKES!

You might be wondering why some of the words in the format appear in italics. It's because they're *placeholders.* A   placeholder is a name, symbol, or formula that you supply. Place-holders are italicized in the format of functions and commands to let you know that you should substitute something at that place in the command.

Here is an example of a `printf()`:

```
printf("I am %d", 16);   /* Prints I am 16 */
```

Because every string in C must be enclosed in quotation marks (as mentioned in Chapter 2), the `controlString` must be in quotation marks. Anything following the `controlString` is optional and is determined by the values you want printed.

 Every C command and function needs a semicolon after it to let C know that the line is finished. Braces and the first lines of functions don't need semicolons because nothing is executing on those lines. All statements with `printf()` should end in a semicolon.

Printing Strings

String messages are the easiest type of data to print with `printf()`. You only have to enclose the string in quotation marks. The following `printf()` prints a message on the screen:

```
printf("Read a lot");
```

When the computer executes this statement, the message Read a lot appears on the screen.

The string Read a lot is the `controlString` in this `printf()`. There is little *control* going on here, just output.

The following two `printf()` statements:

```
printf("Read a lot");
printf("Keep learning");
```

might not produce the output you expect. Here is what the two `printf()`s produce:

```
Read a lotKeep learning
```

PSST!   C does not automatically move the cursor down to the next line when a `printf()` executes. You must insert an *escape sequence* in the `controlString` if you want C to go to the next line after a `printf()`.

Escape Sequences

C contains a lot of *escape sequences,* and you'll use some of them in almost every program you write. Table 4.1 contains a list of some of the more popular escape sequences.

Table 4.1. **Escape sequences.**

Code	Description
\n	Newline
\a	Alarm (the computer's bell)
\t	Tab
\\	Backslash
\"	Quotation mark

YIKES!

The term *escape sequence* sounds harder than it really is. An escape sequence is stored as a single character in C and produces the effect described in Table 4.1. When C sends `'\a'` to the screen, for example, the computer's bell is sounded instead of the characters \ and a actually being printed.

You will see a lot of escape sequences in `printf()` functions. Anytime you want to "move down" to the next line when printing lines of text, you must print `\n` so that C produces a *newline* and moves the blinking cursor down to the next line on the screen. The following `printf()` statements print their messages on separate lines because of the `\n` at the end of the first one:

```
printf("Read a lot\n");
printf("Keep learning");
```

HMM...

The `\n` could have been placed at the beginning of the second line and the same output would have occurred. Because escape sequences are characters to C, you must enclose them in quotation marks so that C knows that the escape sequences are part of the string being printed. The following *also* produces two lines of output:

```
printf("Read a lot\nKeep learning");
```

Because a quotation mark ends a string and because a backslash signals the start of an escape sequence, they have their own escape sequences. `\a` rings your computer's bell, and `\t` causes the output to appear moved over a few spaces. The following `printf()` statements produce the output shown in their comments:

```
printf("Ready\tSet\tGo!\n");        /* Ready    Set    Go! */
printf("Ring my charm!\a\n");       /* Ring my charm! <BEEP> */
```

```
printf("I said, \"No way.\"\n");   /* I said, "No way." */
printf("8\/2 is 4");               /* 8/2 is 4 */
```

  Different C compilers might produce a different number of tabbed spaces for the \t escape sequence.

Conversion Characters

When you print numbers and characters, you must tell C exactly how to print them. You indicate the format of numbers with *conversion characters*. Table 4.2 lists a few of C's most-used conversion characters.

Table 4.2. Conversion characters.

Conversion Character	Description
%d	Integer
%f	Floating-point
%c	Character
%s	String

When you want to print a value inside a string, insert the appropriate conversion characters in the *controlString*. Then, to the right of the *controlString*, list the value you want to be printed. Figure 4.2 is an example of how a `printf()` can print three numbers—an integer, a floating-point value, and another integer.

Figure 4.2.

*printf() conver-
sion characters
determine how
and where
numbers print.*

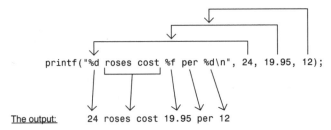

```
printf("%d roses cost %f per %d\n", 24, 19.95, 12);
```

The output: 24 roses cost 19.95 per 12

Strings and characters have their own conversion characters as well. Although you don't need %s to print strings by themselves, you might need %s when printing strings combined with other data. The next printf() prints a different type of data value using each of the conversion characters:

```
printf("%s %d %f %c\n", "Sam", 14, -8.76, 'X');
```

This printf() produces this output:

```
Sam 14 -8.760000 X
```

HMM...   The string Sam needs quotation marks, as do all strings, and the character X needs single quotation marks, as do all characters.

YIKES!

C is crazy when it comes to floating-point numbers. Even though the -8.76 has only two decimal places, C insists on printing six decimal places.

You can control how C prints floating-point values by placing a . between the % and the f of the floating-point conversion character. The following printf() produces four different-looking numbers even though the same floating-point number is given:

```
printf("%f  %.3f  %.2f  %.1f", 4.5678, 4.5678, 4.5678, 4.5678);
```

C rounds the floating-point numbers to the number of decimal places specified in the `%.f` conversion character and produces this output:

```
4.567800  4.568  4.57  4.6
```

PSST!   Just wait! The conversion characters will mean a lot more when you learn about variables in the next chapter.

One last thing: The `printf()` *controlString* controls *exactly* how your output will appear. The only reason two spaces appear between the numbers is that the *constrolString* has two spaces between the `%f`s.

Happy Landings

 Use `printf()` if you want to print data on the screen.

 Every `printf()` requires a control string that determines how your data will look when printed.

 Strings are easy to print. They need no special format codes or conversion characters.

 Use escape sequences to print newlines, tabs, quotes, and backslashes, and to ring the bell.

 Use conversion characters to control how numbers will look.

Shot Down

 Don't expect C to know how to format your data automatically. You must use conversion characters.

 Don't forget `%f`'s decimal control unless you want C to print six decimal places with all floating-point values.

In Review

`printf()` sends data to the screen. A program that can't write to the screen is rarely useful. The programs you write must be able to communicate with the user sitting at the keyboard.

`printf()` requires a *controlString* that describes the format of the data that follows. With the *controlString* you can specify exactly how you want your numbers and character data printed. You also can print escape sequences, which is a fancy name for special output controls that you sometimes need, such as a newline at the end of lines of output.

Code Example

Consider the following partial program listing:

```
printf("%c %s %d %f %.2f\n", 'Q', "Hello!", 14, 64.21, 64.21);
printf("%c\n", 'Q');
printf("%s\n", "Hello!");
printf("%d\n", 14);
printf("%f\n", 64.21);
printf("%.2f", 64.21);
```

Code Analysis

The first `printf()` statement prints five data values—a character, a character string, an integer, a floating-point number, and another floating-point number. The subsequent five lines then print those values one at a time. The last floating-point value's decimal places are specified in the last `printf()` to limit the number of decimal positions printed. Here is the code's output:

```
Q Hello! 14 64.210000 64.21
Q
Hello!
14
64.210000
64.21
```

How Do I Store Stuff?

Using Variables

No doubt you've heard that computers process data. Somehow, you've got to have a way to store that data. In C, as in most programming languages, you store data in *variables*. A variable is nothing more than a box in your computer's memory that holds a number or a character. Chapter 2 explained the different types of data: characters, strings, integers, and floating-points. This chapter explains how to store those types of data inside your program.

Kinds of Variables

There are several different kinds of variables in C because there are several different kinds of data. Not just any variable will hold just any piece of data. Only integers can hold integer data, only floating-point variables can hold floating-point data, and so on.

HMM... Throughout this chapter, think of variables inside your computer as acting like post office boxes in a post office. Post office boxes vary in size and have unique numbers that label each one. Your C program's variables vary in size, depending on the kind of data they hold, and each variable has a unique name that differentiates it from other variables.

The data you learned about in Chapter 2 was called *literal data* (or sometimes, *constant data*). The number 2 and the character 'x' are always 2 and a character 'x'. Lots of data you work with changes. Your age, salary, and weight all change. If you were writing a payroll program, you would need a way to store changing pieces of data. Variables come to the rescue. Variables are little more than boxes in memory that hold values that can change over time.

There are many types of variables. Table 5.1 lists some of the more common types. Notice that many of the variables have data types (character, integer, floating-point, and string) similar to that of literal data. After all, you must have a place to store integers, and you do so in an integer variable.

Table 5.1. Several types of C variables.

Name	Description
char	Holds character data such as `'x'` and `'*'`.
int	Holds integer data such as `1`, `32`, and `-459`. Stores data between –32767 and 32767.
long int	Holds integer data greater than 32767 and less than –32768.
float	Holds floating-point data such as `0.0003`, `-121.34`, and `43323.4`.
double	Holds extremely large and small floating-point data. (`float` can hold only values from -3.4×10^{38} to $+3.4 \times 10^{38}$—that's 3.4 times 10 with 38 zeroes after the 10.)

YIKES!

You might notice that there is no string variable, although there *are* character string literals. C is one of the few programming languages that has no string variables, but as you'll see in Chapter 6, there is a way to store strings in variables.

The *Name* column in Table 5.1 lists the keyword needed when you create variables for programs. In other words, if you want an integer, you need to use the `int` keyword. Before completing your study of variables, you need to know one more thing: how to name them.

Naming Variables

All variables have names, and because you are responsible for naming them, you must learn the naming rules. All variable names must be different. You can't have two variables in the same program with the same name.

A variable can have from 1 to 32 characters in its name. Your program's variables must begin with a letter of the alphabet, but after that letter, variable names can have other letters, numbers, or an underscore in any combination. All of the following are valid variable names:

```
myData    pay93    age_limit    amount    QtlyIncome
```

PSST!   C lets you begin a variable name with an underscore, but you shouldn't do so. Because some of C's built-in variables begin with an underscore, there's a chance you'll overlap one of those if you name your variables starting with underscores.

YIKES!

Don't name a variable with the same name as a function or a command. If you give a variable the same name as a command, your program won't run, and if you give a variable the same name as a function, you can't use that function in your program without causing an error.

Defining Variables

Before you use a variable, you have to *define* it. Variable definition (sometimes called *variable declaration*) is nothing more than letting C know you'll need some variable space so that it can reserve some for you. To define a variable, you only need to state its type, followed by a variable name. Here are the first few lines of a program that defines some variables:

```
main()
{
   char initial;
   int age;
   float amount;
   /* Rest of program would follow */
```

The sample code just presented has three variables—`initial`, `age`, and `amount`. They can hold three different types of data—character data, integer data, and floating-point data. If the program didn't define these variables, it wouldn't be able to store data in the variables.

Skip This, It's Technical

Most C variables are defined after an opening brace, such as the opening brace that follows a function name. These variables are called *local variables*. C also lets you create *global* variables by defining the variables before a function name. Local variables are almost always preferable to global variables. Chapter 28 addresses the differences between local and global variables, but for now, all programs will stick with local variables.

Storing Data in Variables

The *assignment operator* puts values in variables. It's a lot easier to use than it sounds. The assignment operator is simply the equals sign, =. The format of putting data in variables looks like this:

```
variable = data;
```

The `variable` is the variable name that you want to store data in. You must have defined the variable previously, as the preceding section explained. The `data` can be a number, character, or mathematical expression that results in a number. Here are examples of three assignment statements that assign values to the variables defined in the preceding section:

```
initial = 'G';   /* Assigns values to three variables */
age = 31;
amount = 2983.43;
```

You also can store answers to expressions in variables:

```
sales = 4432.67 / 1.20;   /* Divides to get value */
```

and even use other variables in the expression:

```
newSales = sales + 2167.65;   /* Uses value from
                                  another variable */
```

Figure 5.1 gives you an idea of what C does when you use an assignment statement.

PSST! The equals sign tells C this: Take whatever is on the right and stick it into the variable on the left. Oh, and never use commas in numbers, no matter how big the numbers are!

Suppose you were getting paid lots of money to write a payroll calculation program for a small business. You would have to define some floating-point variables to hold the rate being paid per hour, the number of hours worked, the tax rate, and so on. The Blackjack program in Appendix B must keep track of lots of things, and many variables are used there. At the start of most of the program's functions, you'll see a place where variables are being defined.

Figure 5.1.

The assignment operator, =, puts values into variables.

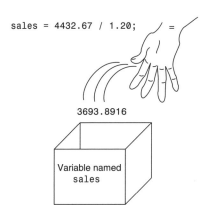

 PSST! You can define variables and give them initial values at the same time. The following code defines three variables and gives initial values to two of them, `val` and `numSold`:

```
int numSold = 25, numBought;
float val = 436.54;
```

Happy Landings

 Learn how to name variables, because you'll have to use them in your programs.

Always define variables before using them.

 The equals sign is called the assignment operator. The assignment operator helps you store values in variables.

Shot Down

 Don't mix data types and variable types. Refrain from storing values of one data type in variables of another data type. The results might confuse you if you mix data types.

 Don't define variables before a function name even though you can. Such variables, called global variables, can cause problems if you're not careful. Instead, define variables after an opening brace of a function. These local variables are safer for you to use for now.

 Don't put commas in numbers. Enter the value thirty thousand as 30000, not as 30,000.

In Review

This chapter taught you a lot about the different types of variables in C. Because there are different kinds of data, we must have different kinds of variables to hold that data. The choice of data types is up to you, the programmer. Choose a variable's data type carefully to ensure that the data type matches any value you will store in that variable.

Don't use a larger data type for a variable when a smaller one is ample to hold the data. Using a long int when a regular int will suffice is not efficient and results in a slower and larger program.

Code Example

```
/* Defines a different variable for each data type */
char priceCode = 'J';
int quantity = 100;
long int wholeSaleQuant = 45000;
float price = 13.54;
double yrlySales = 9845543.23;
```

Code Analysis

The statements in the preceding program section both reserve variable storage and assign initial values to those variables. You don't always have to assign initial values to variables. Many times you don't know the value that a variable will hold because the value will come from the user at the keyboard or from a disk file or a calculation. Whether you know the initial value or not, you still must reserve storage for all your variables before you use them in the program.

Can C Store Words?

In Character Arrays

Although C doesn't have string variables, there is a way to store string data. This chapter explains how. You already know that string data must be enclosed in quotation marks. Even a single character enclosed in quotation marks is a string. You also know how to print strings with `printf()`.

The only task left is to see how to use a special type of character variable to hold string data so that your program can input, process, and output that string data.

"I Am the String Terminator!"

C does the strangest thing to strings: It adds a zero to the end of every string. The zero at the end of strings has several names. Here are some of them:

 Null zero

 Binary zero

 String terminator

 ASCII 0

 \0

YIKES!

About the only thing you *don't* call the string-terminating zero is *zero!* C programmers use the special names for the string-terminating zero so that you'll know that a regular numeric zero or a character `'0'` is not being used at the end of the string.

C marks the end of all strings with the string-terminating zero. You never have to do anything special when entering a string literal such as "My name is Julie." C automatically adds the null zero. You'll never see the null zero, but it is there. In memory, C knows when it gets to the end of a string only when it finds the null zero.

Skip This, It's Technical

If you look at your C compiler's manual, you'll find the ASCII table (discussed in Chapter 2). The very first entry is labeled *null*, and the ASCII number for null is 0. Look further down at ASCII 48, and you'll see a 0. ASCII 48 is the character '0', whereas the first ASCII value is the *null zero*. C puts the null zero at the end of strings. Even the string "I am 20" ends in an ASCII 0 right after the character 0 in 20.

PSST! The string terminator is sometimes called \0 (*backslash zero*) because you can represent the null zero by enclosing \0 in single quotes. Therefore, '0' is the character zero, and '\0' is the string terminator.

Figure 6.1 shows how the string "Crazy" is stored in memory. As you can see, it takes 6 bytes (a *byte* is a single memory location) to store the string, even though the string has only five letters.

Figure 6.1.

A string always ends with a null zero in memory.

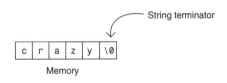

The Length of Strings

The *length* of a string is always the number of characters up to but not including the null zero. There will be times when you need to find the length of a string. The null zero is never counted when determining the length of a string.

Given the definition of the string length, the following strings both have lengths of 9:

`August 10`

and

`Batter up`

YIKES!

The first string's length doesn't end at the 0 in 10 because the 0 in 10 isn't a null zero but a character zero.

 PSST! All single characters of data have a length of 1. Therefore, both `'X'` and `"X"` have lengths of 1, but the `"X"` consumes two characters of memory because of its null zero.

Character Arrays: Lists of Characters

Character arrays hold strings in memory. An *array* is a special type of variable that you'll hear much more about in upcoming chapters.

All the data types—`int`, `float`, `char`, and the rest—have corresponding array types. An array is nothing more than a list of variables of the same data type.

You have to tell C that you need a character array in the same place you would tell C that you need any other kind of variable. Use brackets, [and], after the array name, along with a number indicating the maximum number of characters the string will hold.

An example is worth a thousand words. If you needed a place to hold month names, you could define a character array called `month` like this:

```
char month[10];  /* Defines a character array */
```

PSST! Array definitions are easy. Take away the `10` and the brackets and you have a regular character variable. Adding the brackets with the `10` tells C that you need 10 character variables, each following the other in a list named `month`.

The reason 10 was used when defining the array is that the longest month name, `September`, has nine characters. The tenth character is for—you guessed it—the null zero.

 **HMM...** You *always* have to reserve enough character array space to hold the longest string you will need to hold, plus the string terminator.

If you want, you can store a string value in the array at the same time you define the array:

```
char month[10] = "January";  /* Defines a character array */
```

Figure 6.2 shows you what the array looks like. Because nothing was put in the last two places of the array (January takes only seven characters plus an eighth place for the null zero), you don't know what's in the last two places. (Some compilers, however, fill the unused subscripts with zeroes.)

Figure 6.2.

Defining and initializing an array named month *that holds string data.*

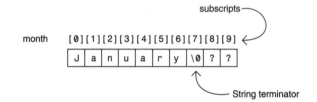

 PSST! Each individual piece of an array is called an *element*. The month array has 10 elements. You can distinguish between them with *subscripts*. Subscripts are numbers that you specify inside brackets that refer to each of the array elements.

All array subscripts begin with 0. As Figure 6.2 shows, the first element in the month array is called month[0]. The last is called month[9] because there are 10 elements altogether, and when you begin at 0, the last will be 9.

Each of the elements in a character array is a character. It is the combination of characters, the array or *list* of characters, that holds the entire string. If you wanted to, you could change the contents of the array from January to March one element at a time, like this:

```
month[0] = 'M';
month[1] = 'a';
month[2] = 'r';
month[3] = 'c';
month[4] = 'h';
month[5] = '\0';   /* Very important */
```

It is vital that you insert the null zero at the end of the string. If you didn't, the `month` array would still have a null zero three places later at `month[7]`, and when you attempted to print the string, you would get this:

```
Marchry
```

  Printing strings in arrays is easy. You can use the `%s` conversion character:

```
printf("The month is %s", month);
```

Skip This, It's Technical

If you define an array *and* initialize the array at the same time, you don't have to put the number in brackets. Both of the following do exactly the same thing:

```
char month[8] = "January";
```

and

```
char month[] = "January";
```

In the second example, C counts the number of characters in January and adds one for the null zero. You won't be able to store a string larger than eight characters later, however. If you want to define a string's character array and initialize it but leave extra padding for a longer string later, you could do this:

```
char month[25] = "January";   /* Leaves room for longer
                                  strings */
```

Initializing Strings

You won't want to initialize a string one character at a time as done in the preceding section. However, unlike with regular non-array variables, you can't assign a new string to the array like this:

```
month = "April";  /* NOT allowed */
```

You can only assign a string to a month with the equals sign *at the time you define the string.* If later in the program you want to put a new string into the array, you must either assign it one character at a time or use C's strcpy() (*string copy*) function that comes with your compiler. The following statement assigns a new string to the month:

```
strcpy(month, "April");  /* Puts new string in month array */
```

PSST! In your programs that use strcpy(), you must put this line after the #include <stdio.h>:

```
#include <string.h>
```

YIKES!

Don't worry. strcpy() automatically adds a null zero to the end of the string it creates.

HMM... The Blackjack game in Appendix B uses a character array to hold the player's first name. See if you can spot which function uses the character array. (It's not main().)

Happy Landings

 Store strings in character arrays.

 Reserve enough array elements to hold the longest string you'll ever store in the character array.

 You can initialize a character array at the time you define the array, assign one element at a time, or use `strcpy()`.

Shot Down

 Don't put a string into a character array unless the character array contains enough elements to hold the string.

 Don't forget that array subscripts begin at 0, not 1.

In Review

Besides storing the numeric data types you read about in Chapter 5, C supplies a way to store character strings also. Unlike single character variables, character strings can hold many characters, such as words, addresses, and paragraphs of text.

C doesn't support a string variable data type. Despite the efficiency obtained by not supporting string variables, programmers can't give up being able to store character string data. Therefore, C offers character arrays that hold several characters of data in string-like form.

Code Example

```
/* Stores the days of the week in seven
   different character arrays */
char day1[7] = "Sunday";
char day2[7] = "Monday";
char day3[8] = "Tuesday";
char day4[10] = "Wednesday";
```

```
char day5[] = "Thursday";
char day6[] = "Friday";
char day7[] = "Saturday";
char myName[6];
strcpy(myName, "Julie");
```

Code Analysis

When you want to store string data, define character arrays as
shown here. You must add brackets after the variable names or C
will think you're defining single-character variables. Always reserve
enough for the null zero that terminates every string. If you assign a
string to the array when you define the array, you don't have to
count the number of characters and add one for the null zero. The
last three day variables do not include the total number of characters because C is able to count the number needed to hold the data
being assigned.

If you want to define an array without assigning data, as done in the
myName array, you must include the maximum number of elements
when you define the array. You then can use strcpy() to assign a
string value to the array.

What Do #include and #define Mean?

They're Preprocessor Directives

Two lines you see in many C programs are not C commands at all. They are *preprocessor directives*. A preprocessor directive always begins with a pound sign, #. Preprocessor directives don't cause anything to happen at runtime (when you run your program). Instead, they do work during the compiling of your program.

The most-often used preprocessor directives are

 `#include`

 `#define`

Including Files

`#include` has two formats, which are almost identical:

`#include <filename>`

and

`#include "filename"`

Figure 7.1 shows what `#include` does. It's nothing more than a *file merge* command. Right before your program is compiled, the `#include` statement is replaced with the contents of the filename specified after `#include`. The `filename` can be stated in either upper-case or lowercase letters as long as your operating system allows for either in filenames (MS-DOS does, but UNIX does not).

PSST!   If you've used a word processor before, you've probably used an `#include` type of command. You might have merged a file stored on disk into the middle of the file you were editing.

Figure 7.1.

#include simply inserts a disk file into the middle of another file.

Here's what you wrote:

Your source file:

```
          :
/* Part of a C program */
age = 31;
printf("I am %d years old" , age);
#include "addr.h"
printf("That's my address");
/*Rest of program follows */
          :
```

The file named addr.h:

```
printf("\n6104 E. Oak\n");
printf("St. Paul, MN\n");
printf("        54245\n");
```

BEFORE

Here's what the compiler sees:

```
          :
/* Part of a C program */
age = 31;
printf("I am %d years old" , age);
printf("\n6104 E. Oak\n");
printf("St. Paul, MN\n");
printf("        54245\n");
printf("That's my address");
/*Rest of program follows */
          :
```

AFTER

When you install your compiler, the installation program sets up a separate location on your disk (in a *directory*) for various #include files that come with your compiler. When you want to use one of these built-in #include files, use the #include format with the angled brackets, < and >.

YIKES!

"How do I know when to use a built-in #include file?" you ask. Good question! All built-in functions, such as printf(), have corresponding #include files. When this book describes a built-in function, it also tells you exactly which file to include.

 PSST! Your compiler manual has a complete list of which functions are included in which files.

HMM... You've already seen two built-in functions—printf() and strcpy(). (main() is not a built-in C function; main() is a function you must supply.) The #include file for printf() is stdio.h (which stands for *standard I/O*), and the #include file for strcpy() is string.h.

PSST! Most C compilers offer *context-sensitive help*. If yours does, you can place the cursor over a built-in function name such as strcpy() and select context-sensitive help (usually by pressing the Alt-F1 key combination). Your compiler tells you in the help message which header file goes with that function.

Almost every complete program listing in this book contains the following preprocessor directive:

```
#include <stdio.h>
```

because almost every program in this book uses printf(). Chapter 6 told you to include string.h because the strcpy() function was discussed.

PSST! The file you include is called a *header file*. That's why most included files end in the extension .H.

If you wrote your own header files, you would use the second form of the preprocessor directive—the one that has quotation marks. If you use quotation marks, C first searches the disk directory in which your program is stored, *then* the built-in #include directory. Because of the search order, you can write your own header files and give them the same name as those built into C, and yours will be used instead of C's.

YIKES!

If you write your own header files, don't put them with C's built-in `#include` file directory. Leave C's supplied header files intact. There is rarely a reason to override C's headers, but you might want to add some additional headers of your own.

HMM...

You might write your own header files when you have program statements you frequently use in many programs. Instead of typing them in every program, you can put them in a file in your program directory and `#include` the file where you want to use the statements.

Where Do I Put #include Directives?

The header files you `#include` are nothing more than text files that contain C code. You will learn much more about the contents of header files later, but for now understand that a header file does two things. The built-in header files help C properly execute built-in functions. The header files you write often contain code that you want to place in more than one file.

PSST!   It's best to put your `#include` directives before `main()`.

The Blackjack program in Appendix B includes lots of header files because it uses lots of built-in functions. Notice the placement of the #includes: They come before main().

Defining Constants

The #define preprocessor directive defines *constants*. A C constant is really the same thing as a literal. You learned in Chapter 2 that a literal is a data value that doesn't change, like the number 4 or the string "C programming". The #define preprocessor directive lets you give names to literals. When you give a name to a literal, the named literal is known in C terminology as a *named constant* or a *defined constant*.

YIKES!

In Chapter 5, you learned how to define variables by specifying their data types and giving them a name and an initial value. Constants you define with #define are *not* variables, even though they sometimes look like variables when they are used.

Here is the format of the #define directive:

```
#define CONSTANT constantDefinition
```

As with most things in C, using defined constants is easier than the format leads you to believe. Here are some sample #define directives:

```
#define AGELIMIT 21
#define MYNAME "Paula Holt"
#define PI 3.14159
```

PSST! In a nutshell, here's what `#define` tells C: Every place in the program that the *CONSTANT* appears, replace it with the *constantDefinition*.

The first `#define` just shown instructs C to find every occurrence of the word `AGELIMIT` and replace it with a 21. Therefore, if this statement appeared somewhere in the program after the `#define`:

```
if (employeeAge < AGELIMIT)
```

the compiler acts as if you typed this:

```
if (employeeAge < 21)
```

even though you didn't.

YIKES!

Use uppercase letters for the defined constant name. This is the one exception in C where uppercase is not only used but recommended. Because defined constants are not variables, the uppercase lets you glance through a program and tell at a glance what is a variable and what is a constant.

PSST! Assuming that you have previously defined the constant `PI`, the uppercase letters help keep you from doing something like this:

```
PI = 544.34;  /* Not allowed */
```

in the middle of the program. As long as you keep defined constant names in uppercase, you will know not to change them because they are *constants*.

Defined constants are good for naming values that might need to be changed between program runs. For example, if you didn't use a defined constant for AGELIMIT, but instead used an actual age limit value such as 21 throughout a program, if that age limit changed, it would be difficult to find and change every single 21. If you had used a defined constant at the top of the program and the age limit changed, you'd only need to change the #define statement to something like this:

```
#define AGELIMIT 18
```

Skip This, It's Technical

The #define directive is not a C command. Just like with #include, C handles your #define statements before your program is compiled. Therefore, if you defined PI as 3.14159, and you used PI throughout a program where you needed the value of the mathematical pi, the C compiler would think *you* typed 3.14159 throughout the program when you really typed PI. PI is easier to remember (and helps eliminate typing mistakes) and is clearer to the purpose of the constant.

Happy Landings

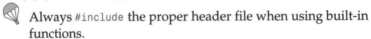 Always #include the proper header file when using built-in functions.

Use angled brackets around the included filename when including compiler-supplied header files.

Use quotation marks around the included filename when including your own header files that you've stored in your source code's directory.

Use uppercase characters in all defined constant names so that you can distinguish them from regular variable names.

Shot Down

 Don't put `#include` statements for the built-in functions after `main()`. `#include` the header files before `main()`. You can `#include` your own header files wherever you want the code inserted.

 Don't treat defined constants as variables. Unlike with variables, you can't store data in a constant once it has been defined.

In Review

C's preprocessor directives make C see code that you didn't actually type. For instance, when you need the contents of another file (such as `stdio.h`) that helps your program produce input and output properly, you don't have to type the contents of that file. You only have to instruct C to include the file via the `#include` directive.

If there is a constant value used throughout your program, such as a sales bonus limit, you should define that constant at the top of the program with `#define`. Instead of typing the actual number throughout the program, you have to type only the constant's name. If the limit ever changes, you have to change only the one `#define` line.

`#include` and `#define` are not C statements that run along with the rest of the program. They work on your source code by including text or changing defined names to actual values before C begins to compile your program.

Code Example

```
#include <stdio.h>
#include "mycode.h"
#define MINORDER 50
#define COMPNAME "Amalgamated Co."
```

Code Analysis

This section of code is composed solely of preprocessor directives. The pound sign (#) in column one is the giveaway. The first line instructs C to copy the `stdio.h` file into the current program. Because angled brackets are used, the regular include directory that was created when you installed your compiler is searched. The second line uses quotation marks around the included file, which instructs C to look in the source program's directory for the file.

Two defined constants, `MINORDER` and `COMPNAME`, are then defined. When the program must later test for or print the minimum order quantity or the company name, the defined constant names are used instead of the constants themselves.

Can I Ask the User Questions?

With scanf()

printf() sends data to the screen. The scanf() function gets data from the keyboard. You must have a way to get data from your user. You can't always assign data values using assignment statements. For example, if you were writing a video rental program for use throughout the country, you couldn't assign the cost of a tape rental to a variable using the equals sign in your program because every store's rental could differ. Instead, you would have to ask the user of the program in each store location how much a tape rental costs before computing a charge.

You will find that scanf() is the *craziest* function that could possibly exist! To a beginner, scanf() makes little sense, but despite its strange format, it is the easiest function to use for input at this point in the book.

Looking at scanf()

Figure 8.1 shows you what scanf() does. scanf() is a built-in C function that comes with all C compilers. Its header file is the same as printf()—stdio.h—so you don't have to worry about including an additional header file for scanf().

Figure 8.1.

scanf() fills variables with values typed by the user.

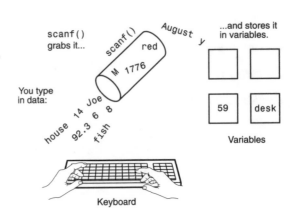

Keyboard

scanf() is fairly easy if you know printf(). scanf() looks a lot like printf() because scanf() uses conversion codes such as %s and %d.

scanf() is the mirror-image function of printf(). Often, you will write programs that ask the user for values with a printf() and get those values with scanf(). Here is the format of scanf():

```
scanf(controlString [, data]);
```

When your program gets to scanf(), C stops and waits for the user to type values. The variables listed inside scanf() (following the controlString) will accept whatever values the user types. scanf() quits when the user presses Enter after typing values.

YIKES!

Even though scanf() uses the same conversion characters as printf(), never specify escape sequences such as \n, \a, or \t. Escape sequences confuse scanf(). scanf() quits getting values from the user when the user presses Enter, so you don't need to specify the \n.

Prompting for scanf()

Almost every scanf() you write should be preceded with printf(). If you don't issue a printf(), the program will stop and wait for input, and the user will have no idea what to do. For example, if you need to get an amount from the user, you would put a `printf()` function like this before `scanf()`:

```
printf("What is the amount? ");  /* Prompt */
/* A scanf() would follow */
```

 PSST! The `printf()` before a `scanf()` is called a *prompt*. If you don't prompt the user for the value or values you want, the user has no way of knowing what values should be typed.

Problems with `scanf()`

One of the first problems with `scanf()` is that although the user must type exactly what `scanf()` expects, the user rarely does this! If the `scanf()` needs a floating-point value, but the user types a character, there is little you can do. The floating-point variable you supply will have bad data because a character is not a floating-point value. For the time being, assume that the user *does* type what is needed. Chapter 18 describes ways to overcome problems brought on by `scanf()`.

 YIKES!

"I have yet to see a `scanf()`. When are you going to show one?" you might be asking. Get ready, because here it comes.

Here is a scanf() that gets an integer value (as you can tell from the %d integer conversion code) from the keyboard into a variable named age:

```
scanf(" %d", &age);
```

The variable age will hold whatever number the user types before pressing Enter.

The first thing to notice about scanf() is the space right before the %d. The space isn't always required here, but it never hurts, and it sometimes helps the input work better when you get numbers and characters in the same program. Adding the extra space is a good habit to get into now.

Enough about all that. Let's get to the most obvious scanf() problem—the ampersand, &, before the variable age. Guess what? scanf() requires that you put the ampersand before all variables, even though the ampersand is *not* part of the variable name! Do it, and scanf() works; leave off the ampersand, and scanf() won't accept the user's values into the variables.

PSST! There is an exception to the ampersand rule you should know about. If you're getting input into a character array using %s, you do *not* use the ampersand.

The bottom-line rule is this: If you're asking the user to type integers, floating-points, characters, doubles, or any of the other single-variable combinations (long integers and so on), put an ampersand before the variable names in the scanf(). If you are asking the user for a string into a character array, don't put the ampersand before the array name.

Skip This, It's Technical

You also wouldn't put the ampersand in front of pointer variables. Actually, an array is nothing more than a pointer variable, and that's why the ampersand isn't needed for arrays. We'll get to pointers later in this book, but if you've seen them in other languages, you know what I'm talking about. If you haven't seen a pointer variable before, and you don't know what this is all about, well, you were warned not to read this paragraph anyway! Seriously, you'll fully understand pointers and how they are like arrays after reading Chapter 23.

HMM... There's a problem with using `scanf()` to get character strings into character arrays that you should know about. `scanf()` stops reading string input at the first space. Therefore, you can get only a single word at a time with `scanf()`.

The following program asks the user for a first name, last name, age, and weight. Notice that the character arrays have no ampersands, but that the other two variables do. The program doesn't ask for the user's full name because `scanf()` isn't capable of getting two words at once.

```
#include <stdio.h>
main()
{
   int age;
   float weight;
   char first[15], last[15];
```

```
      printf("\nWhat is your first name? ");
      scanf(" %s", first); /* No ampersand on character arrays */
      printf("What is your last name? ");
      scanf(" %s", last);  /* No ampersand on character arrays */

      printf("How old are you? ");
      scanf(" %d", &age);  /* Ampersand required */
      printf("How much do you weigh? ");
      scanf(" %f", &weight);

      printf("\nHere is the information you entered:\n");
      printf("Name: %s %s\n", first, last);
      printf("Weight: %.0f\n", weight);  /* 0 decimal places */
                                         /* wanted          */
      printf("Age: %d", age);
      return 0; /* Always best to use this. I'll explain later */
   }
```

Here is a sample execution of this program:

```
What is your first name? Joe
What is your last name? Harrison
How old are you? 41
How much do you weigh? 205

Here is the information you entered:
Name: Joe Harrison
Weight: 205
Age: 41
```

  You can let the user type characters other than data values, but you have to trust the user to type things just right. Here is a scanf() that gets a date and expects the user to type the date in *mm/dd/yy* format:

```
scanf(" %d/%d/%d", &month, &day, &year);
```

The user could type 02/28/94 or 11/22/95 but not June 5th, 1993 because the scanf() is expecting something else.

Happy Landings

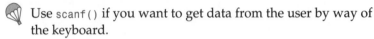

Use `scanf()` if you want to get data from the user by way of the keyboard.

Every `scanf()` requires a control string that dictates how your data will look when input.

Before using a `scanf()`, use a `printf()` to prompt the user for the values you want.

Put an ampersand before non-array variables in a `scanf()`.

Shot Down

Don't use an ampersand in front of array names in a `scanf()`.

Don't expect the user to type exactly what you want! If exact accuracy is needed, such as in an end-user environment where noncomputerists will be using your program, you'll want to use other means of input that are explained in Chapter 18.

In Review

This chapter's goal was to teach you how to ask for and get answers from the user. Being able to process user input is an important part of any language. `scanf()` gets user input and stores that input in variables. Although `scanf()` uses the same format codes as `printf()`, `scanf()` has extra requirements that you should understand. `scanf()` requires an & in front of non-array variables. Also, if you are getting strings from the user, the `scanf()` and `%s` combination can get only one word at a time.

Code Example

```
/* Asks users for their hometown, state, and year born */
printf("What town were you born in? ");
scanf(" %s", homeTown);   /* homeTown must be a
                              character array */
printf("What state were you born in? ");
scanf(" %s", state);   /* state must be a character array */
printf("What year were you born in? ");
scanf(" %d", &yearBorn);   /* yearBorn must be numeric */
```

Code Analysis

These lines of code prompt the user with a `printf()` before each `scanf()`. With the printed prompts, the user knows exactly what is required. The format code must match the variable's data type. Earlier in the program, the variables `homeTown` and `state` must have been defined as character arrays. The variable `yearBorn` is an `int` data type. (`int` is large enough to hold year values.)

Because the first two variables are arrays, no ampersand is needed before them in the `scanf()`s. An `&` *is* needed before non-array variables such as `yearBorn`.

How Does C Do Math?

With Operators

There are two kinds of operators. There are the ones you talk to on the phone, but we won't be discussing those. There are also C operators, which let you do math. You don't have to be a math wizard to write programs that use math operators. C does all the math for you as long as you know how to list the operators properly.

Not only should you learn to recognize math operators, but you should also learn how C orders math operators. C doesn't always calculate from left to right. This chapter explains why.

The Basics

Lots of C operators work exactly the way you expect them to. You use a plus sign, +, when you want to add, and you use a minus sign, -, when you want to subtract. An *expression* includes one or more operators. C programmers often use math expressions on the right side of the assignment operator when filling variables with values, like this:

```
totalSales = localSales + foreignSales - salesReturns;
```

C computes the answer and then stores that answer in `totalSales`.

PSST!   If you want to subtract a negative value, be sure to put a space between the minus signs, like this:

```
newValue = oldValue - -factor;
```

You can even put a math expression inside a `printf()`:

```
printf("In 3 years, I'll be %d years old.\n", age + 3);
```

If you want to multiply and divide, you can do so by using the *
and / symbols. The following statement assigns a value to a variable
using multiplication and division:

```
newFactor = fact * 1.2 / 0.5;
```

YIKES!

If you put integers on *both* sides of the division symbol, C
computes the *integer division result.* Study the following
expressions to get used to integer division and regular division.
The comments explain the results calculated from the divisions:

```
float a = 17.0;
float b = 5.0;
float answf;
int i = 17;
int j = 5;
int answi;
answf = a / b;  /* 3.4 is stored in answf */
answi = i / j;  /* 3 is stored in answi */
```

HMM... If you need the remainder after integer division, use
C's *modulus* operator, %. Given the values just listed,
the following statement puts a 2 in ansMod:

```
ansMod = i % j;  /* 2 is the remainder of 17 / 5 */
```

You now know the three ways C divides values: regular division if a
noninteger is on either or both sides of the /, integer division if an
integer is on both sides of the /, and modulus if the % operator is
used between two integers.

PSST!   You can't use % between anything but integer data types.

Order of Operators

As mentioned earlier in this chapter, C doesn't always compute math operations in the order you expect. The following expression explains it in a nutshell:

```
ans = 5 + 2 * 3;  /* Puts 11 in ans */
```

If you thought that C would store 21 in ans, you're reading the expression from left to right. However, C always computes multiplication before addition! It sounds crazy, but as long as you know the rules, you'll be okay. C is following the *order of operators* table. C first multiplies 2 and 3 to get 6, then adds 5 to get 11.

Fun Fact
The first computer bug was a real bug. A military printer wouldn't work because a moth was caught between two wires.

You'll find the complete order of operators table in the tear-out card of this book. As you can see in the table, *, /, and % appear before + and -. Therefore, if C sees an expression with a combination of these operators, it evaluates *, /, and % before computing + and -.

Here is a difficult expression. Assume that the variables and numbers are integers. See if you can figure out the answer the way C would evaluate the expression:

```
ans = 5 + 2 * 4 / 2 % 3 + 10 - 3;  /* What is answer? */
```

The answer, 13, is found in Figure 9.1.

Figure 9.1.

*Solving the
expression the
way C would.*

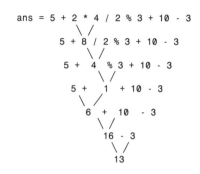

```
ans = 5 + 2 * 4 / 2 % 3 + 10 - 3
           \ /
      5 + 8 / 2 % 3 + 10 - 3
            \ /
        5 +  4  % 3 + 10 - 3
              \ /
          5 +  1  + 10 - 3
           \ /
             6  + 10  - 3
               \ /
                16 - 3
                  \ /
                   13
```

PSST!   Don't do too much at one time when evaluating such
expressions for practice. As the figure shows, you should
compute one operator at a time, then bring the rest of the
expression down for the next round.

If an expression such as the one in Figure 9.1 contains more than one
operator that sits on the same level in the order of operators table,
you must use the third column, labeled Associativity, to determine
how the operators are evaluated. In other words, because *, /, and %
all reside on the same level, they were evaluated from left to right,
as dictated by the order of operators table's Associativity column.

You might wonder why you have to learn this stuff. After all,
doesn't C do your math for you? The answer is "Yes, *but...*" C does
your math, but you need to know how to set up your expressions
properly. The classic reason is as follows: Suppose you want to
compute the average of four variables. The following will *not* work:

```
avg = i + j + k + l / 4;   /* Will NOT compute average! */
```

The reason is simple once you understand the order of operators. C
computes the division first, so l / 4 is evaluated first, then i, j, and
k are added to that divided result. If you want to override the order
of operators, as you'd have to do in this case, you have to learn to
use ample parentheses around expressions.

Break the Rules with Parentheses

If you need to override the order of operators, you can. If you group an expression inside parentheses, C will evaluate that expression before the others. Because the order of operators table shows parentheses before any of the other math operators, parentheses have precedence, as the following statement shows:

```
ans = (5 + 2) * 3;  /* Puts 21 in ans */
```

Even though multiplication is usually performed before addition, the parentheses force C to evaluate 5 + 2 first and then multiply the resulting 7 by 3. Therefore, if you want to average four values, you can do so by grouping the addition of the values in parentheses:

```
avg = (i + j + k + l) / 4;  /* Computes average */
```

 PSST!   Use lots of parentheses. They clarify your expressions. Even if the regular operator order will suffice for your expression, parentheses will make the expression easier for you to decipher if you need to change the program later.

Assignments Everywhere

As you can see from the order of operators table, the assignment operator has precedence and associativity, as do the rest of the operators. Assignment has very low priority in the table, and it associates from right to left.

The right-to-left associativity lets you perform an interesting operation: You can assign a value to more than one variable in the same expression. To assign a 9 to 10 variables, you *could* do this:

```
a = 9; b = 9; c = 9; d = 9; e = 9;
f = 9; g = 9; h = 9; i = 9; j = 9;
```

but this is easier:

```
a = b = c = d = e = f = g = h = i = j = 9;
```

C first assigns the 9 to j because of the right-to-left associativity, then puts the 9 in i, and so on.

PSST! C doesn't initialize variables for you. If you wanted 0 put in a bunch of variables, a multiple assignment would do it for you.

Skip This, It's Technical

Every C expression produces a value. The expression j = 9; does put a 9 in j, but it also results in a completed value of 9, which is available to store somewhere else if needed. The fact that every assignment results in an expression lets you do things like this that you can't always do in other programming languages:

```
a = 5 * (b = 2);   /* Puts a 2 in b and a 10 in a */
```

Happy Landings

 Use +, -, *, and / for addition, subtraction, multiplication, and division.

 Use % if you want the remainder of an integer division.

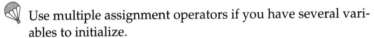

Keep the order of operators table handy, because it determines how C evaluates expressions.

Use multiple assignment operators if you have several variables to initialize.

Shot Down

 Don't put two minus signs together if you want to subtract a negative number. Leave a space between them.

 Don't use % to compute the remainder of noninteger data division. If you divide nonintegers, the result will be an accurate floating-point answer.

In Review

C provides lots of math operators that do calculations for you. Most of the operators look like their math counterparts (+, -, /, and so on), and the others are easy to learn. The primary consideration you must concern yourself with is the order of operators. C's order of operators table shows you the way C interprets the order of your calculations. You can use parentheses to override that built-in order if you like.

Code Example

```
total = cost * numberBought;
sTax = .08 * total;
grandTotal = total + sTax;
discounted = grandTotal - .10 * grandTotal;
```

Code Analysis

This series of assignment statements computes the total sale amount and the discount amount of a purchase. The cost of each item is first multiplied by the number of items bought. An 8 percent tax must be taken out of the total, then added back in. A 10 percent discount is computed from the grand total if the customer pays cash.

No parentheses are needed in any of the calculations because the natural order of operators works for the example. If you'd like to make the order even clearer, you could add parentheses, such as in this rewritten last statement:

```
discounted = grandTotal - (.10 * grandTotal);
```

Part 2
The Operating Room

Call 911, Carol!
She's about to blow!

What Else Can I Do with Expressions?

Combine Operators and Give Typecasts

As you can see from the order of operators table on the tear-out card, C has a rich assortment of operators. It is the fact that C has many operators that helps C keep its command vocabulary small. There aren't many commands in C, but there are a lot more operators than in most other programming languages.

This chapter explores a few more operators that you'll need as you write programs. The compound assignment operators and the typecast operator provide the vehicles for several advanced operations.

Compound Assignment

There are many times in your programs when you will have to change the value of a variable. Until now, all variables have been assigned values based on constant literal values or expressions. However, there will often be times when you must update a variable.

Suppose your program had to count the number of times a profit value goes below zero. You would need to set up a *counter variable*. A counter variable is just a variable that you add one to when a certain event takes place. Every time a profit value goes negative, you might do this:

```
lossCount = lossCount + 1;   /* Adds 1 to lossCount variable */
```

YIKES!

In math, nothing can be equal to itself plus 1! In computers, though, the previous assignment statement first adds 1 to lossCount, then assigns that new value to lossCount— in effect adding 1 to lossCount's value.

There will be other times when you need to update a variable by adding to a total or by adjusting it in some way. The following assignment statement increases the variable sales by 25 percent:

```
sales = sales * 1.25;  /* Increases sales by 25 percent */
```

C provides several *compound operators* that let you update a variable in a manner similar to the methods just described. However, instead of repeating the variable on *both* sides of the equals sign, you have to list the variable only once. As with much of C, some examples will help clarify what is done with the compound operators.

If you want to add 1 to a variable, you can use the *compound addition* operator, +=. These two statements are exactly the same thing:

```
lossCount = lossCount + 1;  /* Adds 1 to lossCount variable */
```

and

```
lossCount += 1;  /* Adds 1 to lossCount variable */
```

Instead of multiplying sales by 1.25 and then assigning it to itself like this:

```
sales = sales * 1.25;  /* Increases sales by 25 percent */
```

you can use the *compound multiplication* operator, *=, to do this:

```
sales *= 1.25;  /* Increases sales by 25 percent */
```

HMM... The compound operators are quicker to use because you don't have to list the same variable name on both sides of the equals sign. Also, the compound operators reduce typing errors because you don't have to type the same variable name twice in the same statement.

Table 10.1 lists all the compound assignment operators and gives examples of each. All of the operators you've seen so far in this book, from addition through modulus, have corresponding compound operators.

Table 10.1. **Compound assignment operators.**

Compound Operator	Example	Equivalent Statement
*=	total *= 1.25;	total = total * 1.25;
/=	amt /= factor;	amt = amt / factor;
%=	days %= 3;	days = days % 3;
+=	count += 1;	count = count + 1;
-=	adjust -= 0.5;	adjust = adjust - 0.5;

 **HMM...** The dispCard() function in the Blackjack game in Appendix B uses a compound addition operator to update the card count depending on the value of the last card drawn.

Watch That Order!

Take a quick glance at the order of operators table and locate the compound assignment operators. You'll see that they have very low precedence. The +=, for instance, is lower by several levels than the +.

At first, this might not sound like a big deal. (Actually, maybe none of this sounds like a big deal. If so, *great!* C should be easier than a lot of people would have you think.) The order of operators table can haunt the unwary C programmer. Think about how you would evaluate the second of these expressions:

```
total = 5;
total *= 2 + 3;   /* Updates the total variable */
```

At first glance, you might think that the value of `total` is 13 because multiplication is done before addition. You're right that multiplication is done before addition, but *compound multiplication* is done *after* addition according to the order of operators. Therefore, the 2 + 3 is evaluated to get 5, and *then* that 5 is multiplied by the old value of `total` (which also happens to be 5) to get a total of 25, as Figure 10.1 points out.

Figure 10.1.

The compound operators reside on a low level.

```
total * = 2+3;
```
is the same thing as this:
```
total = total *(2 + 3);
```
because * = is lower than + In the table.

Typecasting: Hollywood Could Take Lessons from C

There are two kinds of typecasting. There is the kind that directors of movies often do, but we'll not cover that here. There is also C's typecasting. A C *typecast* temporarily changes the data type of one variable to another. Here is the format of a typecast:

```
(dataType)value
```

The *dataType* can be any C data type such as int, float, and so on. The *value* is any variable, literal, or expression. Suppose that age is an integer variable that holds 6. The following:

```
(float)age
```

converts age to a float value of 6.0. If you were using age in an expression with other floats, you should typecast age to float to maintain consistency in the expression.

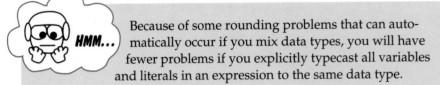

Because of some rounding problems that can automatically occur if you mix data types, you will have fewer problems if you explicitly typecast all variables and literals in an expression to the same data type.

Never use a typecast on a line by itself. Typecast where a variable or an expression has to be converted to another value to properly compute a result. The preceding typecast of age might be represented like this:

```
salaryBonus = salary * (float)age / 150.0;
```

age does *not* change to a floating-point variable! age is changed only *temporarily* for this one calculation. Everywhere in the program that age is not explicitly typecast, it is still an int variable.

  If you find yourself typecasting the same variable to a different data type throughout a program, you might have made it the wrong type to begin with.

Skip This, It's Technical

You can typecast an entire expression.
The following statement typecasts the result
of an expression before assigning it to a variable:

```
value = (float)(number - 10 * yrsService);
```

The parentheses around the expression keep the typecast
from casting only the variable number.

Happy Landings

 Use compound assignment operators when updating variable values.

 Use compound assignment operators to eliminate a few typing errors and to decrease your program-writing time.

Put a data type in parentheses before a variable, expression, or data value you want to typecast.

Shot Down

Don't mix data types. Instead, typecast data so that it is all the same type before evaluating it.

Don't ignore the order of operators! The compound operators have low priority in the table and are done after almost every other operator finishes.

In Review

The goal of this chapter was to teach you additional operators that help you write C programs. Use the compound operators when you want to change the value of a variable. You don't have to repeat the variable name on both sides of the equals sign because a compound operator understands that you want to update the variable's value. (This saves you lots of typing and potential errors if you use long variable names such as `costOfGoodsSold`.)

If you want to mix variables and constants of different data types, use typecasting to produce uniform data types in expressions. Although C will typecast automatically, you won't always like the results. C might convert `float` to `int` when you wanted everything to remain `float`. Typecasting becomes especially critical later when you write more advanced programs that use pointers and structures.

Code Example

```
int age;
float dogAge;
printf("How old are you? ");
scanf(" %d", &age);  /* Gets the user's age as an integer */
dogAge = (float)age / 7.0;
printf("If you were a dog, you'd only be %.1f years old!",
       dogAge);
```

Code Analysis

The code first asks the user for his or her age. Because people rarely enter fractional ages, the age value is stored in an integer variable. The age is then divided by 7.0 to get the corresponding age in dog years. (A year to a dog is like seven years to a person, which makes you wonder how Lassie has lived since the 1950s.)

Because the division produces a floating-point result, the typecast ensures that `age` is converted to `float` before the calculation is performed. Making your data types consistent is very important as you move into more advanced programming.

Can I Compare Two Values?

With Relational Operators

C provides an extremely useful statement called if. if lets your programs make decisions and execute certain statements based on the results of those decisions. By testing contents of variables, your programs can produce different output given different input.

Relational operators are also described in this chapter. Relational operators, combined with if, make C a powerful data-processing language. Computers would really be boring if they couldn't test data! Computers would be little more than calculators if they had no capability to decide courses of action based on data.

Testing Data

C's if statement works just like it does in spoken language: *If something is true, do one thing; otherwise, do something else.* Consider these statements:

> If I make enough money, we'll go to Italy.
> If the shoes don't fit, take them back.
> If it's hot outside, water the lawn.

Table 11.1 lists C's relational operators, which permit testing of data.

Table 11.1. C's relational operators.

Relational Operator	Description
==	Equal to
>	Greater than
<	Less than
>=	Greater than or equal to
<=	Less than or equal to
!=	Not equal to

 **HMM...** Relational operators compare two values. You always put a variable, literal, or expression—or a combination of any two of them—on either side of a relational operator.

Before delving into `if`, let's look at a few relational operators and see what they really mean. A regular operator produces a mathematical result. A relational operator produces a *true* or *false* result. When you compare two data values, the data values either produce a true comparison or they don't. For example, given the following values:

```
int i = 5;
int j = 10;
int k = 15;
int l = 5;
```

the following statements are *true:*

```
i == l
j < k
k > i
j != k
```

The following statements are *not* true, so they are *false:*

```
i > j
k < j
j == l
```

Fun Fact
To tell the difference between = and ==, remember that you need two equals signs to double-check whether something is equal.

YIKES!

Only like values should go on either side of the relational operator. In other words, don't compare a character to a float. If you have to compare two unlike data values, use a typecast to keep the values the same data type.

Every time C evaluates a relational operator, a value of 1 or 0 is produced. True always results in 1, and false always results in 0. The following statements would assign a 1 to the variable a and a 0 to the variable b:

```
a = (4 < 10);  /* (4 < 10) is true, so a 1 is assigned */
b = (8 == 9);  /* (8 == 9) is false, so a 0 is assigned */
```

You have seen only the beginning of relational operators. The next section explains in more detail how to use them.

Using if

The if statement uses relational operators to perform data testing. Here's the format of the if statement:

```
if (condition)
   { block of one or more C statements; }
```

The parentheses around the *condition* are required. The *condition* is a relational test like those described in the preceding section. The *block of one or more C statements* is called the *body* of the if statement. The braces around the *block of one or more C statements* are required if the body of the if contains more than a single statement.

PSST!   Even though braces aren't required if an if contains just one statement, always use the braces. If you later add statements to the body of the if, the braces will be there.

Here is an if statement:

```
if (age < 18)
   { printf("You cannot vote yet\n");
     yrs = 18 - age;  /* Calculates how many years
                         until the user can vote   */
     printf("You can vote in %d years.\n", yrs); }
```

The if reads like this to the C programmer: "If the variable named age contains a value less than 18, print the messages and calculate the value of yrs. Otherwise, don't print and calculate. Whatever happens, the program continues at the statement that follows the body of the if."

> **HMM...** The main() function in the Blackjack program in Appendix B asks the player if he or she wants to hit or stand (in casino lingo, that means to draw another card or not). An if is used to determine exactly what the user wants to do.

Otherwise...: Using else

In the preceding section, you saw how to write a course of action that executes if the relational test is true. If the relational test were false, nothing happened. This section explains the else statement that you can add to if. Using else, you can specify exactly what happens when the relational test is false. Here is the format of the combined if-else:

```
if (condition)
   { block of one or more C statements; }
else
   { block of one or more C statements; }
```

Here is an example of if-else:

```
if (age < 18)
   { printf("You cannot vote yet\n");
     yrs = 18 - age;
       /* Prints an appropriate message,
           depending on user's age */
     printf("You can vote in %d years.\n", yrs); }
else
   { printf("You've made it to adulthood.\n"); }
```

If the age is less than 18, the body of the if executes. If the age is *not* less than 18, the body of the else executes.

PSST!   Put semicolons only at the end of executable statements in the body of the if or the else. Never put a semicolon after the if or the else. Semicolons go only at the end of complete statements.

HMM...   As with the body of the if, the body of the else doesn't require braces if it consists of a single statement, but it's a good idea to use braces anyway.

Happy Landings

 Use relational operators to compare data.

 Remember that a true relational result produces a 1 and a false relational result produces a 0.

 Use if to compare data and else to specify what to do if the if test fails.

 Put braces around the if body of code and around the else body of code.

Shot Down

 Don't put values of different data types on each side of a relational operator.

 Don't put a semicolon after `if` or `else`. Semicolons go only at the end of each statement, inside the body of the `if` or the `else`.

In Review

The goal of this chapter was to show you ways to test data and execute one set of code or another depending on the result of that test. You don't always want the same code to execute every time someone runs a program. Computers must be able to look at data and process that data (which is why it's called *data processing*).

The relational operators and the `if` statement work together to produce a true or false analysis of data.

Code Example

```
printf("How much did you make last year? ");
scanf(" %f", &salary);
if (salary > 100000.0)
    { printf("Wow! You really worked hard despite ");
      printf("what some might think!"); }
else
    {   sal100 = 100000.0 - salary;
        printf("Only $%.0f more to reach the century mark!",
                sal100); }
```

Code Analysis

When the user enters a salary, the program makes a decision depending on the salary's relation to $100,000. If the user earned more than $100,000 (we should all be so productive!), a congratulatory message is printed. If the user earned less than $100,000, a message prints telling the user how far away from $100,000 he or she is. (Most of us have quite a way to go!)

The `else` statement ensures that only one set of code or the other after `if` executes.

How Do I Test Several Things at Once?

With Logical Operators

Sometimes the relational operators described in Chapter 11 simply can't express all testing conditions. For example, if you wanted to test whether a numeric or character variable is within a certain range, you would have to use two `if` statements, like this:

```
if (age >= 21) {   /* See if 21 <= age <= 65 */
  if (age <= 65)   {
     printf("You are within range.\n");
  }
}
```

Although there's nothing wrong with using nested `if` statements, they're not extremely straightforward, and their logic is slightly more complex than you really need. By using the *logical operators* you'll read about in this chapter, you can combine more than one relational test in a single `if` statement to clarify your code.

Getting Logical

There are three logical operators (see Table 12.1). Sometimes logical operators are known as *compound relational operators* because they let you combine more than one relational operator.

Table 12.1. The logical operators.

Logical Operator	Meaning
&&	And
||	Or
!	Not

Logical operators appear between two or more relational tests. For example, here are the first parts of three `if` statements that use logical operators:

```
if ((age >= 21) && (age <= 65)) {
```

and

```
if ((hrsWorked > 40) ¦¦ (sales > 25000.00)) {
```

and

```
if (!(isCharterMember)) {
```

PSST! If you combine two relational operators with a logical operator, or if you use the ! (not) operator to negate a relation, the *entire* expression following the `if` statement requires parentheses.

Of course, there is more to the preceding `if` statements than what is shown, but the `if` bodies aren't shown because you know what they would look like.

Logical operators work just as they do in regular spoken English. For example, consider the spoken statements that correspond to the code lines just seen:

```
if ((age >= 21) && (age <= 65)) {
    /* If the age is at least 21 and no more than 65,... */
if ((hrsWorked > 40) ¦¦ (sales > 25000.00)) {
    /* If the hours worked are more than 40 or the sales are
       more than $25000,... */
if (!(isCharterMember)) {
    /* If you aren't a charter member, you must... */
```

As you have no doubt figured out, these three spoken statements describe exactly the same tests done by the three `if` statements shown earlier. You often place an *and* between two conditions, such as "If you take out the trash *and* clean your room, you can play."

HMM...   Reread that stern statement you might say to a child. The and condition places a strict requirement that both of the jobs must be done before the result can take place. That's what `&&` does also. Both sides of the `&&` must be true in order for the body of the `if` to execute.

Let's continue with this same line of reasoning for the `||` (or) operator. You might be more lenient on the kid by saying this: "If you take out the trash *or* clean your room, you can play." The or is not as restrictive. One side or the other side of the or must be true (and they both can be true as well). If either side is true, the result can occur. The same holds for the `||` operator. One or the other side of the `||` must be true (or they both can be true) in order for the body of the `if` to execute.

The `!` (not) operator reverses a true or a false condition. True becomes false and false becomes true. This sounds confusing, and it is! Limit the number of `!` operators you use. You can always rewrite a logical expression to avoid using `!` by reversing the logic.

PSST!   Suppose you wanted to write an inventory program that tests whether the number of a certain item has fallen to zero. The first part of the `if` might look like this:

```
if (count == 0) {
```

Because the `if` is true *only* if `count` has a value of 0, you can rewrite the statement like this:

```
if (!count) {  /* Executes if's body only if
                count is 0 */
```

YIKES!

Again, the ! adds a little confusion to code. Even though you might save some typing effort with a fancy !, clearer code is better than trickier code. `if (count == 0) {` is probably better to use, despite the microsecond your program might save by using !.

Using the && operator, the following program prints one message if the user's last name begins with the letters P through S, and another message if the name begins with something else.

```
#include <stdio.h>
main()
{
   char name[25];
   printf("What is your last name? ");
   scanf(" %s", name);

   if ((name[0] >= 'P') && (name[0] <= 'S'))
      { printf("You must go to room 2432 ");
        printf("for your tickets.\n"); }
   else
      { printf("You can get your tickets here.\n"); }
   return 0;  /* Leaves the program to DOS or C editor */
}
```

HMM...

How would the program be different if the && were changed to a ||? Would the first or the second message appear? The answer is the first one. *Everybody* would be sent to room 2432. Any letter from A to Z is either more than P or less than S. The test in the preceding program has to be && because room 2432 is available only to those people whose names are between P and S.

PSST! You can combine more than two relational operators with logical operators, but doing too much in a single statement can cause confusion. This is a little much:

```
if ((a < 6) ¦¦ (c >= 3) && (r != 9) ¦¦ (p <= 1)) {
```

The Order of Logical Operators

Because logical operators appear in the order of operators table, they have priority at times, just as the other operators do. Studying the order of operators will show you that the && operator has precedence over the ¦¦. Therefore, the following logic:

```
if (age < 20 ¦¦ sales < 1200 && hrsWorked > 15) {
```

is interpreted by C like this:

```
if ((age < 20) ¦¦ ((sales < 1200) && (hrsWorked > 15))) {
```

Use ample parentheses. Parentheses help clarify the order of operators. C won't get confused if you don't use parentheses, because it knows the order of operators table very well. However, a person looking at your program has to figure out which is done first, and parentheses help group operations together.

PSST! The Blackjack game in Appendix B uses && and ¦¦ to determine the winning hands in the findWinner() function. Even though a lot of the program is still new to you, you should be able to read through this function's logic and get a glimpse of what's happening.

Happy Landings

  Use logical operators to connect relational operators.

  Use && when both sides of the operator have to be true in order for the entire condition to be true.

  Use ¦¦ when either one side or the other side (or both) have to be true in order for the entire condition to be true.

Shot Down

  Don't overdo the use of !. Most negative logic can be reversed (< can become >=) to get rid of the not operator.

  Don't combine too many relational operators in a single expression.

In Review

This chapter's goal was to teach you the logical operators. Although relational operators test data, the logical operators, && and ¦¦, let you combine more than one relational test into a single statement and execute code accordingly.

As you saw in this chapter, we often use logical-like operators in real life. Often, we make decisions based on several conditions.

Code Example

```
printf("What is your grade average for last semester? ");
scanf(" %f", &avg);
printf("How many hours did you take? ");
scanf(" %d", &hours);
if ((avg > 90.0) && (hours > 15))
   { printf("You are a top-notch student!\n");
     printf("Keep up the good work!"); }
```

Code Analysis

The code's intention is to give good students encouragement. These two relations are tested: the student's grade-point average and the number of hours the student took. The grade-point average alone is not enough to encourage the student because the student might have taken only a single course. Just because the student took a lot of courses doesn't mean the student excelled, either.

Therefore, *both* the grade-point average and the number of hours taken are combined into one compound relational test using the && operator. If the student's average is good *and* the student took a lot of courses, the student is encouraged to continue.

Are There More Operators?

Additional C Operators

Have patience! You've learned about almost all of the C operators. With the exception of a few more advanced operators that you'll read about in Chapter 23, this chapter rounds out the order of operators table and exs *conditional operators, increment operators,* and *decrement operators.*

C's operators sometimes substitute for more wordy commands that you'd use in other programming languages. Not only can an assortment of operators speed your program development time, they also compile more efficiently and run faster than commands. The C operators do a lot to make C the efficient language that it is.

Good-Bye if-else; Hello Conditional

The conditional operator is the only C operator that requires *three* arguments. Whereas division, multiplication, and the rest require two values to work, the conditional operator requires three. Although the format of the conditional operator looks complex, you will see that it streamlines some logic and is actually straightforward to use.

The conditional operator looks like this: `?:`. Here is its format:

```
relation ? trueStatement : falseStatement;
```

The `relation` is any relational test such as `age >= 21` or `sales <= 25000.0`. You also can combine the relational operators with the logical operators you learned about in Chapter 12. The `trueStatement` is any valid C statement, and the `falseStatement` is also any valid C statement. Here is an example of a conditional operator:

```
(total <= 3850.0) ? (total *= 1.10): (total *= 1.05);
```

PSST! The parentheses are not required, but they do help group the three parts of the conditional operator so that you can see them easier.

If the test in the first set of parentheses is true, the `trueStatement` executes. If the test in the first set of parentheses is false, the `falseStatement` executes. The conditional operator you just saw does *exactly* the same thing as this `if-else` statement:

```
if (total <= 3850.0)
   { total *= 1.10; }
else
   { total *= 1.05; }
```

HMM... Just about any `if-else` statement can be rewritten as a conditional statement. The conditional requires less typing, you won't accidentally leave off a brace somewhere, and the conditional runs more efficiently than an `if-else` because it compiles into more compact code.

PSST! The format of the conditional operator is obvious when you think of it like this: The question mark asks a question. Keeping this in mind, you could state the earlier example as follows: *Is the total <= 3850.0? If so, do the first thing; otherwise, do the second.*

This statement tells C to multiply `total` by 1.10 or by 1.05, depending on the result of the relational test.

Don't replace every single `if-else` with a conditional operator. Sometimes `if-else` is more readable, and some things are just too complex to squeeze easily into a conditional operator. However, when a simple `if-else` is all that's needed, the conditional operator provides a nice alternative.

The conditional operator offers one additional advantage over `if`: The conditional often can appear in places where `if` can't go. The following `printf` prints a trailing `s` if the number of pears is more than one:

```
printf("The %d pear%s", numPear, (numPear>1) ? ("s.") : ("."));
```

If the value in `numPear` is greater than 1, you'll see something like this printed:

```
The 4 pears.
```

but if there is only one pear, you'll see this:

```
The 1 pear.
```

> **HMM...** Maybe you're wondering why the conditional operator is ?:, but the question mark and colon *never* appear next to each other. Well, that's just the way it is. It would be too cumbersome to go around saying that the conditional operator looks like a question mark and a colon with some stuff in between.

The Small-Change Operators: ++ and --

Whereas the conditional operator works on three arguments, the *increment* and *decrement* operators work on only one. The increment operator adds 1 to a variable, and the decrement operator subtracts 1. That's it, 'nuff said. Almost....

Incrementing and decrementing variables are things you'd need to do if you were counting items (such as the number of customers who shopped in your store yesterday) or counting down (such as removing items from an inventory as people buy them). The increment operator is ++ and the decrement operator is --. If you want to add one to the variable count, here's how you do it:

```
count++;
```

You also can do this:

```
++count;
```

The decrement operator does the same thing, only the 1 is subtracted from the variable. The operators can go on either side of the variable. If the operator is on the left, it's called a *prefix increment* or *prefix decrement*. If the operator is on the right, it's known as a *postfix increment* or *postfix decrement*.

YIKES!

Never apply an increment or decrement operator to a literal constant or an expression. Only variables can be incremented or decremented.

Prefix and postfix produce identical results when used by themselves. It is only when you combine them with other expressions that a small "gotcha" appears. Consider the following code:

```
int i = 2, j = 5, n;
n = ++i * j;
```

The question is, what is n when the statements finish executing? It's easy to see what's in j because j doesn't change and still holds 5. i is always incremented, so you know that i is 3 afterwards. The trick is determining exactly when i increments. If i increments before the multiplication, n becomes 15, but if i increments after the multiplication, n becomes 10.

The answer lies in the *prefix* and *postfix* placements. If the ++ or -- is *prefix*, C computes it before anything else on the line. If the ++ or -- is *postfix*, C computes it after everything else on the line finishes. Because the ++ in the preceding code is prefix, i increments to 3 before being multiplied by j. The following statement increments i *after* multiplying i by j and storing the answer in n:

```
n = i++ * j;   /* Puts 10 in n and 3 in i */
```

Being able to increment a variable in the same expression as you use the variable means less work on the programmer's part.

Skip This, It's Technical

The ++ and -- operators are extremely efficient. If you care about such things (most of us don't), ++ and -- compile into only one machine language statement, whereas adding or subtracting 1 using + 1 or − 1 doesn't always compile so efficiently.

Sizing Up the Situation

Fun Fact
sizeof() *doesn't look like an operator at all. It looks (and acts) like a function call.*

You use sizeof() to find the number of memory locations it takes to store values of any data type. Although most C compilers use 2 bytes to store integers, not all do. To find out for sure exactly how much memory is being used by integers and floating points, you can use sizeof(). The following statements do just that:

```
i = sizeof(int);    /* Puts size of integers into i */
f = sizeof(float);  /* Puts size of floats into f */
```

If you need to know how much memory variables and arrays take, you can apply the sizeof() operator to them also. The following section of code shows you how:

```
char name[] = "George Paul";
int i = 7;
printf("The size of i is %d\n", sizeof(i));
printf("The size of name is %d", sizeof(name));
```

YIKES!

Although sizeof() might seem worthless right now, you'll see how it comes in handy as you progress in C.

PSST! The length of a string and the size of a string are two different values. The length is the number of bytes up to but not including the null zero, and it is found via strlen(). The size of a string is the number of characters it takes to hold the string, including the null zero.

Happy Landings

 Use the conditional operator in place of simple if-else statements to improve efficiency.

 The conditional operator requires three arguments. Extra parentheses help clarify these three arguments.

 Use ++ and -- to increment and decrement variables instead of adding and subtracting 1.

Shot Down

 Don't duplicate assignment statements on each side of the conditional operator's :. Pull the variable and the assignment operator completely out of the conditional operator and place them on the left of the conditional to improve efficiency.

 Don't think that prefix and postfix produce the same values. Prefix and postfix are identical only when a single variable is involved. If you combine ++ or -- with other variables and expressions, the placement of *prefix* and *postfix* is critical to get the result you want.

In Review

The goal of this chapter was to round out your knowledge of C's operators and show you most of the ones remaining to be learned.

The longest C operator, ?:, and the shortest C operators, -- and ++, were taught. Understanding these operators doesn't take a lot of work, yet the operators are powerful and substitute for complete statements in other languages. One of C's operators doesn't look like an operator at all. The sizeof() operator returns the number of memory locations consumed by whatever is in its parentheses.

Code Example

```
if (age < 18)
   { gift = 5.00; }
else
   { gift = 10.00; }
gift = (age < 18) ? 5.00 : 10.00;   /* Does the same
                                        as the if */
age++;   /* Adds 1 to age */
printf("In a year, you'll be %d years old.\n", age);
intSize = sizeof(int);
printf("Integers take %d memory locations.", intSize);
```

Code Analysis

The first part of this code is redundant. If you were to remove the if statement, the program would perform exactly the way it does with the if. The conditional operator does the same thing in one statement that the if does in four. The conditional operator assigns a gift of either $5 or $10, depending on the age of the user.

One is then added to the user's age so that users can see their age a year from now (as if they couldn't do this themselves!). Lastly, the code prints a message telling the user how much memory is taken up by integers on the machine running the program.

Part 3
Keeping Control

That silly machine always chickens
out during the loop-the-loop!

How Can I Do the Same Stuff Over and Over?

With while and do-while Loops

Now that you've learned the operators, you're ready to play "loop-the-loop" with your programs. A *loop* is simply a section of code that repeats a few times. You don't want a loop to repeat forever. That's called an *infinite loop*. The loops you write (if you write them properly, and of course you will) should come to a conclusion when they finish doing the job you set them up to do.

Why would you want a program to loop? The answer becomes clear when you think about the advantage of using a computer for tasks that people wouldn't want to do. Computers never get bored, so you should give them mundane and repetitive tasks and leave the tasks that require thought to people. You wouldn't want to pay someone to add a list of hundreds of payroll figures, and few people would want to do it anyway. Computer programs can do that kind of repetitive work. People can then analyze the results when the computer loop finishes calculating all the figures.

If you want to add a list of figures, print company sales totals for the past 12 months, or add up the number of students who enroll in a computer class, you need to use a loop. This chapter explains two common C loops that use the `while` command.

while We Repeat

The `while` statement always appears at the beginning or the end of a loop. The easiest type of loop that uses `while` is called the `while` loop. (The other is called the `do-while` loop. You'll see it a little later.) Here is the format of `while`:

```
while (condition)
   { block of one or more C statements; }
```

The `condition` is a relational test that is exactly like the relational test `condition` you learned for `if`. The `block of one or more C statements` is called the *body* of the `while`.

PSST! The body of the while repeats as long as the *condition* is true. Remember how the if works: The body of the if executes if the *condition* is true. The body of the if executes only once, however, whereas the body of the while can execute lots of times.

Figure 14.1 helps explain the similarities and differences between if and while. The formats of the two commands are similar in that braces are required if the body of the while has more than one statement. Also, never put a semicolon after the while's parenthesis. The semicolon follows only the statements inside the body of the while.

Figure 14.1.

The if body executes once, and the while body can repeat more than once.

```
Using if:
  if(amount < 25)
    {
    printf("Amount is too small.\n");
    wrongVal++; MOVE ALONG
    }
```
Executes only one time but only then if amount is less than 25.

```
Using while:
  while (amount < 25)
    {
    printf("Amount is too small.\n");

    wrongVal++;

    printf("Try again...What is new amount?");

    scanf("%d",&amount); GO BACK
    }
```
Keeps repeating as long as amount is less than 25.

YIKES!

The two statements in Figure 14.1 are similar, but they don't do the same thing. while and if are two separate statements that do two separate things.

You *must* somehow change a variable inside the while loop's *condition*. If you don't, the while will loop forever because it will test the same *condition* each time through the loop. Therefore, you avoid infinite loops by making sure the body of the while loop changes something in the *condition* so that eventually the *condition* will become false and the program will continue with the statements that follow the while loop.

HMM... As with if, the while might *never* execute! If the *condition* is false going into while the first time, the body of the while doesn't execute.

Using while

If you want to repeat a section of code until a certain condition becomes false, while is the way to go. The Blackjack program in Appendix B contains a slick use of while in the dispTitle() function to clear the screen. It is repeated here for your review:

```c
/* Clears everything off the screen */
void dispTitle(void)
{
   int i = 0;
   while (i < 25)      /* Clears screen by printing 25 blank */
    { printf("\n");    /* lines to "push off" stuff that      */
      i++; }           /* might be left over on the screen    */
                       /* before this program                 */
   printf("\n\n*Step right up to the Blackjack tables*\n\n");
   return;
}
```

Skip This, It's Technical

Almost every C compiler has a built-in function that clears the screen. The problem is that none of these screen-clearing functions are compatible with the ANSI C standard. Therefore, I used another method to erase the screen before each Blackjack game. A while loop prints 25 newlines. When the cursor gets to the bottom of a screen, the screen scrolls upward, and what was on the screen gets pushed off the top. This simple and generic screen-clearing function, written using while, works with all ANSI C compilers, such as the one you probably have.

HMM... The looping method for screen clearing is not really elegant, but it's about the most generic way possible to clear the screen. If you want to dig through your compiler's manual and replace this while loop with your compiler's screen-clearing function, go ahead.

Back to the actual while code needed to clear the screen: The variable i is initially set to 0. The first time while executes, i is less than 25, so the while condition is true and the body of the while executes. In the body, a newline is sent to the screen and i is incremented. The second time the condition is tested, i has a value of 1, but 1 is still less than 25, so the body executes again. The body continues to execute until i is incremented to 25. Because 25 is not less than 25 (they are equal), the condition becomes false and the loop stops repeating. The rest of the program is then free to execute.

PSST!   If i were not incremented in this screen-clearing `while`, the
`printf()` would execute forever or until you pressed Ctrl-
Break to stop it.

Using do-while

`while` also can be used in conjunction with the `do` statement. When
used as a pair, the statements normally are called `do-while` statements or the `do-while` loop. The `do-while` behaves almost exactly like
the `while` loop. Here is the format of `do-while`:

```
do
    { block of one or more C statements; }
while (condition)
```

PSST!   The `do` and `while` act like wrappers around the body of the
loop. Again, braces are required if the body has more than
a single statement.

Use a `do-while` in place of a `while` only when the body of the loop
must execute at least one time. The *condition* is located at the *bottom* of
the `do-while` loop, so C can't test the *condition* until the loop finishes
the first time.

The Blackjack program asks the user if he or she wants to hit (that's
casino lingo for drawing another card) or stand by asking the user
to type an H or an S. However, users don't always type what they're
supposed to. Therefore, when you request user input that has a
fixed number of possibilities, such as an H or an S, you should check
what the user enters to make sure it's one of the answers you're
expecting. Here is a sample `do-while`, similar to that used in the

Blackjack program, that keeps asking the user for an answer until the user gets it right:

```
do {
    ans = getAns("Hit or stand (H/S)? ");
} while ((ans != 'S') ¦¦ (ans != 'H'));   /* Loop if bad
                                             answer */
```

The strange-looking `getAns()` function call simply executes a function that displays the `Hit or stand (H/S)?` message and gets a character from the user into `ans`. For now, study the formation of the `do-while` because that is the center of your concern here.

PSST! Chapter 19 explains how to test for an uppercase Y or N or a lowercase y or n with a built-in function.

Happy Landings

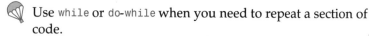 Use `while` or `do-while` when you need to repeat a section of code.

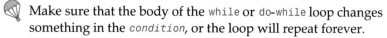 Make sure that the body of the `while` or `do-while` loop changes something in the *condition*, or the loop will repeat forever.

Remember that loops differ from `if` because the body of an `if` executes only once instead of lots of times if the *condition* is true.

Shot Down

 Don't put a semicolon after the `while` *condition*'s closing parenthesis. If you do, an infinite loop will occur.

 Don't assume that the user will answer questions the way you expect. Keep asking for an answer until the user types what you need.

In Review

The goal of this chapter was to show you how to repeat sections of code. The while and do-while loops both repeat statements within their statement bodies. All code between the while and do-while braces repeats instead of executing only once. Both the while and do-while statements cause their code sections to repeat while a given relational condition is true.

The difference between the two statements lies in the placement of the relational test that controls the loops. The while statement tests the relation at the top of the loop, and the do-while statement tests the relation at the bottom of the loop, forcing all its statements to execute at least once.

Code Example

```
ctr = 1;
while (ctr <= 20)
    { printf("%d \n", ctr);
      ctr++; }
ctr = 1;
do
    { printf("%d \n", ctr);
      ctr++; }
while (ctr <= 20);
```

Code Analysis

The code shows both kinds of loops presented in this chapter. The program prints the numbers from 1 to 20 twice. The first half of the program uses while to control the loop, and the second half uses do-while to control the loop. As you can see, both kinds of loops can do the very same thing. The choice of while and do-while is often trivial. You would choose one over the other only when the first cycle was important and you wanted the loop to execute at least once (with do-while) or maybe not at all.

Are There Other Loops?

The for Loop

There is another type of C loop called the `for` loop. A `for` loop offers more control than `while` and `do-while`. With a `for` loop you can specify exactly how many times you want to loop, whereas you must continue looping as long as a condition is true with `while` loops.

There is room for all three kinds of loops in C programs. There are times when one fits a program's requirements better than another. For example, if you wrote a program to handle customer orders as customers purchase items from the inventory, you would need to use a `while` loop. The program would process orders *while* customers came through the door. If 100 customers happened to buy things, the `while` loop would run 100 times. At the end of the day you might want to add the 100 customer purchases to get a total for the day. You could then use a `for` loop because you would then know exactly how many times to loop.

HMM... By incrementing counter variables, you can simulate a `for` loop with a `while` loop. You also can simulate a `while` with a `for`! Therefore, the kind of loop you use ultimately depends on which kind you feel comfortable with at the time.

for Repeat's Sake!

Despite the lame title of this section, the `for` loop is important for controlling repeating sections of code. The format of `for` is a little strange:

```
for (startExpression; testExpression; countExpression)
   { block of one or more C statements; }
```

Perhaps a short example with actual code would be easier to understand:

```
for (ctr = 1; ctr <= 10; ctr++)
   { printf("Still counting... ");
     printf("%d.\n", ctr);
   }
```

Here's the way this for statement works: When the for begins, the *startExpression*, which is ctr = 1;, executes. The *startExpression* is executed *only once* in any for loop. The *testExpression* is then tested. In this example, the *testExpression* is ctr <= 10;. If it is true, and it will be true the first time in this code, the body of the for loop executes. When the body of the loop finishes, the *countExpression* is executed (ctr is incremented).

YIKES!

That's a lot to absorb in one fell swoop — even in one paragraph. Let's make it easy. Follow the line in Figure 15.1, which shows in what order for executes. While following the line, reread the preceding paragraph. It should then make more sense to you.

Figure 15.1.

Following the order of for.

```
for(ctr=1;ctr <=10;ctr++)

   {printf("Still counting...");

   printf("%d.\n", ctr);

   }
```

HMM... The `for` loop's format is strange because of the embedded semicolons that are required. It is true that semicolons go only at the end of executable statements, but statements inside `for` loops *are* executable. For instance, the initial expression, `ctr = 0;`, is completed before the loop begins, as Figure 15.1 shows.

Here is the very same loop written as a `while` statement:

```
ctr = 1;
while (ctr <= 10)
   { printf("Still counting... ");
     printf("%d.\n", ctr);
     ctr++;
   }
```

Here is the output of this code:

```
Still counting...1
Still counting...2
Still counting...3
Still counting...4
Still counting...5
Still counting...6
Still counting...7
Still counting...8
Still counting...9
Still counting...10
```

PSST! If you follow Figure 15.1's guiding line and read the preceding `while` loop too, you'll see how the `for` and `while` do the same thing. The `ctr = 1;` that precedes the `while` is the first statement executed in the `for`.

The do-while loop can't really represent the for loop because the relational test is performed *before* the body of the for loop and after in the do-while. The do-while's test, as you might recall from the end of Chapter 14, always resides at the bottom of the loop.

HMM...

Working with for

The for loop reads a lot like the way you speak in everyday life. Consider this statement:

> For each of our 45 employees, calculate the pay and print a check.

This statement leaves no room for ambiguity. There will be 45 employees, 45 pay calculations, and 45 checks printed. for loops don't always count *up* as the preceding one did with ctr. Here is a for loop that counts *down* before printing a message:

```
for (cDown = 10; cDown > 0; cDown--)
   { printf("%d\n", cDown); }
printf("Blast off!\n");
```

Here is the output of this code:

```
10
9
8
7
6
5
4
3
2
1
Blast off!
```

Fun Fact
If you were programming in BASIC or QBasic, you'd need a next *for each* for *statement. In C, you don't!*

PSST!   If the last expression in the `for` parentheses decrements in some way, the initial value must be greater than the test value in order for the loop to execute. In the previous `for` statement, the initial value of 10 is greater than the `testExpression`'s 0 comparison.

The following `for` loop counts up by 3s, beginning with 1:

```
for (i = 1; i < 22; i += 3)
   { printf("%d ", i); }   /* Prints 1, 4, 7, 10, 13, 16, 19 */
```

The following code produces an interesting effect:

```
for (outer = 1; outer <= 3; outer++)
  { for (inner = 1; inner <= 5; inner++)
      { printf("%d ", inner);
      }
  }          /* Prints 1 2 3 4 5 1 2 3 4 5 1 2 3 4 5 */
```

If you put a `for` loop in the body of another loop, you are *nesting* the loops. In effect, the inner loop executes as many times as the outer loop dictates. You might need a nested `for` loop if you wanted to print three lists of your top five customers. The outer loop would move from one to three, while the inner loop would print the top five customers.

The Blackjack game in Appendix B uses a `for` loop to initialize 52 cards. Here is the code that does that:

```
for (sub = 0; sub <= 51; sub++)  {  /* Counts from 0 to 51 */
   val = (val == 14) ? 1 : val; /* If val is 14, reset to 1 */
   cards[sub] = val;
   val++;  }
```

You have yet to learn about arrays (a special kind of variable list, which is what `cards[]` is), but you can see that the `for` loop counts up, starting at 0, until `sub` is equal to 51 (for 52 cards total). The line with the long `?:` conditional operator ensures that `val` never goes higher than 14. Four sets of numbers from 1 to 14 (making a total of 52) are assigned to the initial card deck. The numbers 1 through 14 indicate cards from the Ace to the King.

Happy Landings

 Use a `for` loop when you want to increment or decrement a variable through a loop.

 Remember that the `for` loop's relational test is performed at the top of the loop.

Use a nested loop if you want to loop a certain number of times.

Shot Down

Don't forget the semicolons inside the `for` loop. `for` requires them.

Don't use an initial value that is greater than the test value if you want to count down with `for`.

In Review

The goal of this chapter was to show you one additional way to form a loop of statements in C. The `for` statement gives you a little more control over the loop than either `while` or `do-while`. The `for` statement controls a loop with a variable that is initialized and changed according to the expressions in the `for` statement.

Code Example

```
for (chap = 1; chap <= 15; chap++)
   { printf ("You're done with Chapter %d \n", chap); }
```

Code Analysis

Here's what the code produces:

```
You're done with Chapter 1
You're done with Chapter 2
You're done with Chapter 3
    :
```

and so on until the message You're done with Chapter 15 prints. The for statement causes the loop control variable chap to increment from its initial value of 1 to its final value of 15. Once chap becomes larger than 15, the for statement terminates the loop and the program continues from there.

What if I Want to Stop in the Middle of a Loop?

Use **break** and **continue**

This chapter doesn't teach you how to use another kind of loop. Instead, this chapter extends the information you learned in the last two. There are ways to control the `while` loop in addition to a relational test, and you can change the way a `for` loop operates via means other than the counter variable.

The `break` and `continue` statements let you control loops for those special occasions when you want to quit a loop early or repeat a loop sooner than it would normally repeat.

Take a break

The `break` statement rarely, if ever, appears on a line by itself. Typically, `break` appears in the body of an `if` statement. The reason will be made clear shortly. Here is the format of `break`:

```
break;
```

YIKES!

`break` is easy, isn't it? Yep, not much to it. However, keep in mind that `break` usually resides in the body of an `if`. In a way, `if` is the first part of almost every `break`.

`break` always appears inside a loop. The `break` statement terminates the current loop. When a loop ends, the code following the body of the loop takes over. When `break` appears inside a loop's body, `break` terminates that loop immediately and the rest of the program continues.

Here is a `for` loop that normally would print 10 numbers. Instead of 10, however, the `break` causes the loop to stop after printing five numbers.

```
for (i = 0; i < 10; i++)
   { printf("%d ", i);
     if (i == 4)
        { break; }  /* Quits loop after i becomes 4 */
   }
/* Rest of program goes here */
```

As a real-world example, suppose a teacher wrote a program to average her 25 students' test scores. The following program keeps a running total of the 25 students. If, however, a student or two missed the test, the teacher wouldn't want to average the entire 25 student scores. If the teacher enters a –1.0 for a test score, the –1.0 triggers the break statement and the loop terminates early.

```
#include <stdio.h>
main()
{
   int numTest;
   float stTest, avg, total = 0.0;
   /* Asks for up to 25 tests */
   for (numTest = 0; numTest < 25; numTest++)
     { printf("What is the next student's test score? ");
       scanf(" %f", &stTest);
       if (stTest < 0.0)
          { break; }  /* Quits early if no more students */
       total += stTest;
     }
   avg = total / numTest;
   printf("\nThe average is %.1f%%.\n", avg);
   return 0;  /* Exits the program */
}
```

Before we discuss the program, take a look at a sample run of it:

```
What is the next student's test score? 89.9
What is the next student's test score? 92.5
What is the next student's test score? 51.0
What is the next student's test score? 86.4
What is the next student's test score? 78.6
What is the next student's test score? -1

The average is 79.7%.
```

Fun Fact
Now that you know about the break *statement, you can use it to get out of infinite loops.*

The teacher had a lot of sick students that day! If all 25 students had shown up, the for loop would have ensured that exactly 25 test scores were asked for. However, because only five took the test, the teacher had to let the program know, via a negative number in this case, that she was done entering the scores and that she now wanted an average.

PSST!

To get the percent sign at the end of the final average, two %s have to be used in the printf() control string. C interprets a percent sign as a control code unless you put two of them together, as done in this program.

YIKES!

break simply offers an early termination of a while, do-while, or for loop. break can't exit from if, which isn't a loop statement. Figure 16.1 helps show the action of break.

Figure 16.1.

break terminates a loop earlier than usual.

```
printf("How many numbers do you want to see?");
scanf("%d",&num);
for (i=1; i<10;i++)
    {
    printf("Counting up...\n");
    if (i== num)
        {break;}
    }
/* Rest of program follows*/
```

Normal flow of the loop

If break executes

Let's continue Working

Whereas break causes a loop to *break* early, continue forces a loop to *continue* early. (So *that's* why they're named that way!) Depending on the complexity of your for, while, or do-while loop, you might not want to execute the *entire body of the loop every iteration.* continue says, in effect, "C, please ignore the rest of this loop's body this iteration of the loop. Go back up to the top of the loop and start the next loop cycle."

YIKES!

The word *iteration* is a fancy computer name for the cycle of a loop. Programmers sometimes think they will keep their jobs if they use words that nobody else understands.

The following program shows off continue nicely. The program contains a for loop that counts from 1 to 10. If the loop variable contains an odd number, the message I'm rather odd... prints and the continue instructs C to ignore the rest of the loop body because it prints Even up! for the even numbers that are left.

```
#include <stdio.h>
main()
{  int i;
   for (i = 1; i <= 10; i++)
     { if ((i%2) == 1)  /* i is odd if true */
       { printf("I'm rather odd...\n");
         continue;
       }
         printf("Even up!\n"); }

   return 0;  /* Exits the program */
}
```

Here is the program's output:

```
I'm rather odd...
Even up!
I'm rather odd...
Even up!
I'm rather odd...
Even up!
I'm rather odd...
Even up!
I'm rather odd...
Even up!
```

PSST! As with break, continue is rarely used without a preceding if statement of some kind. If you *always* wanted to continue, you wouldn't have entered the last part of the loop's body. You want to use continue only in some cycles of the loop.

YIKES!

Look again at how the preceding program knew that the loop variable was odd. The remainder of a variable divided by 2 is always 1 for odd numbers and 0 for even ones.

Happy Landings

 Use break to terminate for, while, or do-while loops early.

 Use continue to force a new cycle of a loop.

Shot Down

 Don't use break or continue without some sort of relational test before them.

In Review

The goal of this chapter was to teach you how to better control loops
with the `break` and `continue` statements. The `while`, `do-while`, and `for`
loops can all be terminated early with `break` or continued early with
`continue`. Although you will want many of the loops you write to
execute until their natural conclusions, you need to change the way
they loop or stop looping.

Code Example

```c
for (i = 1; i < 100; i++)
   {
   printf ("Testing %d\n", i);
   /* Checks whether the number is divisible by 3 AND 4 */
   if ((i % 3 == 0) && (i % 4) == 0) {
      printf ("Found it!\n");
      break; }
   /* Checks whether the number is divisible by 3 */
   if (i % 3 == 0) {
      printf ("I am divisible by 3.\n");
      printf ("But that's only half the test!\n");
      continue; }
   /* Checks whether the number is divisible by 4 */
   if (i % 4 == 0) {
      printf ("I am divisible by 4.\n");
      printf ("One out of two isn't bad!\n");
      continue; }
   printf ("I'm not divisible by 3 or 4!\n");
   }
```

Code Analysis

The code presented here cycles through the numbers from 1 to 100
and reports the first number that is divisible by both 3 and 4 (called
the *least common denominator*). If the number is divisible by 3 only or
divisible by 4 only, a message is printed saying so, and the loop (via
`continue`) cycles again. The `break` statement toward the top of the
loop forces the early conclusion of the `for` statement if the number
is found to be divisible by 3 and 4.

How Can I Test Lots of Values?

With the **switch** Statement

The if statement is great for simple testing of data, especially if your data tests have only two or three possibilities. You can use if to test for more than two values, but if you do, you have to nest several if statements inside one another, and that can get confusing and hard to maintain.

Consider for a moment how you execute code based on a user's response to a menu. A menu is a list of options from which to select, such as this one:

```
What do you want to do?
    1. Add information
    2. Change information
    3. Print information
    4. Delete information
    5. Quit the program
What is your choice?
```

It would take four if-else statements, nested inside one another, to handle all these conditions. There is nothing wrong with nested ifs, but the C switch statement is better for multiple conditions.

Making the switch

The switch statement has one of the longest formats of any statement in C (or just about any other language). Here is the format of switch:

```
switch (expression)
    { case (expression1): { one or more C statements; }
      case (expression2): { one or more C statements; }
      case (expression3): { one or more C statements; }
        /* If there are more case statements,
            they would go here                  */
      default: { one or more C statements; }
    }
```

YIKES!

As with most statements, the actual use of switch is a lot less intimidating than its format leads you to believe.

The menu shown earlier is perfect for a series of function calls. The problem is that this book has yet to discuss function calls except for a handful of built-in functions such as printf() and scanf(). The following simple switch statement prints an appropriate message, depending on the choice the user makes:

```
/* Menu printing statements go here */
do
{  printf("What is your choice? ");
   scanf(" %d", &choice);
   switch (choice)
   { case (1) : printf("You are adding.\n");
               break;
     case (2) : printf("You are changing.\n");
               break;
     case (3) : printf("You are printing.\n");
               break;
     case (4) : printf("You are deleting.\n");
               break;
     case (5) : exit(1);  /* Quits program.
                              Requires stdlib.h */
               break;
     default  : printf("I don't know the ");
               printf("option %d.\n", choice);
               printf("Try again.\n");
   }
} while ((choice >= 1) && (choice <= 5));
/* Rest of program would follow */
```

The case statements determine a course of action based on the value of choice. For example, if choice equals 2, the message You are changing. prints. If choice equals 5, the program quits using the built-in exit() function.

Skip This, It's Technical

Anytime you need to terminate a program before its natural conclusion, use the `exit()` function. The value you place in `exit()`'s parentheses will be returned to your operating system. Most beginning programmers ignore the return value and put either a 0 or 1 in the parentheses. You must `#include stdlib.h` in every program that uses `exit()`.

The `do-while` loop keeps the user honest. If the user enters something other than a number from 1 to 5, the `I don't know` message prints thanks to the `default` keyword. C ensures that if none of the other cases matches the variable listed after `switch`, the `default`'s statements execute.

HMM... `default` works like `else` in a way. `else` takes care of an action if an `if` test is false, and `default` takes care of an action if none of the other `case` conditions successfully matches the `switch` variable.

PSST! The `switch` variable can be either an integer or a character variable. Do not use a `float` or a `double` for the `switch` test.

break and switch

The `switch` statement shown earlier has several `break` statements scattered throughout the code. The `break`s ensure that only one `case` executes. Without the `break` statements, the `switch` would "fall through" to the other `case` statements. Here is what would happen if the `break` statements were removed from the `switch` and the user answered with a `choice` of 2:

```
You are changing.
You are printing.
You are deleting.
```

The `break` keeps `switch case` statements from running together.

The only reason the `default` condition's message did not print is that the `exit()` function executed inside `case (5)`.

Efficiency Considerations

`case` statements don't have to be arranged in any order. Even `default` doesn't have to be the last `case` statement. As a matter of fact, the `break` after the `default` statement isn't needed as long as `default` appears at the end of `switch`. However, putting `break` after `default` helps ensure that you move both statements if you ever rearrange the `case` statements. If you were to put `default` higher in the order of `case` statements, `default` would require a `break` so that the rest of the `case` statements wouldn't execute.

PSST! The reason you might rearrange the `case` statements is efficiency. Put the most-common `case` possibilities toward the top of the `switch` statement so that C won't have to search down into the `case` statements to find a matching `case`.

The `dispCard()` function in the Blackjack program in Appendix B uses a `switch` to print face cards and update the points in each hand.

Happy Landings

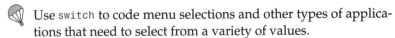 Use `switch` to code menu selections and other types of applications that need to select from a variety of values.

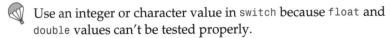 Use an integer or character value in `switch` because `float` and `double` values can't be tested properly.

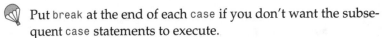 Put `break` at the end of each `case` if you don't want the subsequent `case` statements to execute.

Shot Down

 Don't use nested `if` statements when a `switch` statement will work instead. `switch` is a clearer statement.

In Review

The goal of this chapter was to explain C's `switch` statement. `switch` analyzes the value of an integer or character variable and executes one of several sections of code called *cases*. You can write equivalent code using embedded `if` statements, but `switch` is clearer, especially when your program needs to analyze a user's response to a menu and execute sections of code accordingly.

Code Example

```
printf("Are you filing a single, joint, or ");
printf("married return (s, j, m)? ");
do
{  printf("What is your choice? ");
   scanf(" %c", &choice);
```

```
   switch (choice)
   { case ('s') : printf("You get a $1,000 deduction.\n");
                  break;
     case ('j') : printf("You get a $3,000 deduction.\n");
                  break;
     case ('m') : printf("You get a $5,000 deduction.\n");
                  break;
     default    : printf("I don't know the ");
                  printf("option %d.\n", choice);
                  printf("Try again.\n");
   }
} while ((choice != 's') && (choice != 'j') &&
                            (choice != 'm'));
/* Rest of program would follow */
```

Code Analysis

The code first asks the user a question with three possible answers. Depending on the result of the answer, s, j, or m, the program prints an appropriate tax-related message.

A switch statement should always be written to handle the unexpected. The default case takes over if the user enters anything other than s, j, or m, and the do-while ensures that the question keeps being asked until the user answers with one of the three answers.

How Else Can I Control Input and Output?

With Built-In I/O Functions

There are more ways to produce input and output than the scanf() and printf() functions. This chapter shows you some of C's built-in I/O functions that you can use to control I/O. You can use these simple functions to build powerful data-entry routines of your own.

These functions offer the *primitive* ability to input and output one character at a time. Of course, you also can use the %c format specifier with scanf() and printf() for single characters, but the character I/O functions explained here are a little easier to use, and they provide some capabilities that scanf() and printf() don't offer.

putchar() and getchar()

getchar() gets a single character from the keyboard, and putchar() sends a single character to the screen. Figure 18.1 shows you what happens when you use these functions. They work basically the way you think they would. You can use them just about anytime you want to print or input a single character into a variable.

Figure 18.1.

Use getchar() and putchar() to input and output single characters.

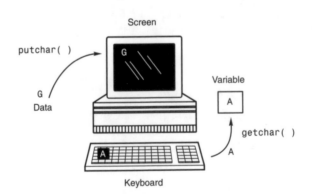

PSST!   Always include the stdio.h header file when using this chapter's I/O functions, just as you do for printf() and scanf().

HMM... The name `getchar()` sounds like "get character," and `putchar()` sounds like "put character." Looks as though the designers of C knew what they were doing!

The following code prints `C is fun` a character at a time using `putchar()` to print each element of the character array in sequence. Notice that `strlen()` is used to ensure that the `for` doesn't output past the end of the string.

```
#include <stdio.h>
#include <string.h>
main()
{
    int i;
    char msg[] = "C is fun";
    for (i = 0; i < strlen(msg); i++)
        { putchar(msg[i]); }  /* Outputs a single character */
    putchar('\n');  /* Must do because putchar() doesn't */
    return 0;  /* All done */
}
```

The `getchar()` function returns the character input from the keyboard. Therefore, you usually assign the character to a variable or you do something else with it. You can put `getchar()` on a line by itself like this:

```
getchar();  /* Does nothing with the character you get */
```

but most C compilers warn you that this statement is rather useless. The `getchar()` function would get a character from the keyboard, but then nothing would be done with the character.

YIKES!

The Blackjack program in Appendix B contains a `getchar()` on a line by itself in `getAns()`. Believe it or not, this is not necessarily inconsistent with the preceding paragraph. You'll see why in a few moments.

Here is a program that gets a character at a time from the keyboard and stores them in a character array. A series of `putchar()` functions then prints the array backwards.

```c
#include <stdio.h>
#include <string.h>
main()
{   int i;
    int msg[25];
    for (i = 0; i < 25; i++)
        { msg[i] = getchar();  /* Gets a character at a time */
          if (msg[i] == '\n')
              { break; }  /* Quits if user presses Enter */
        }
    putchar('\n');  /* Prints a blank line */
    for (; i >= 0; i--)
        { putchar(msg[i]); }  /* Prints a character at a time */
    putchar('\n');
    return 0;  /* All done */
}
```

PSST! Notice that the second `for` loop variable `i` has no initial value! Actually, it does. `i` contains the last array subscript entered in the previous `getchar()`'s `for` loop.

YIKES!

The input character typically is defined as an `int`, as done here. Integers and characters are about the only C data types you can use interchangeably without worry of typecasts. In some advanced applications, `getchar()` can return a value that won't work in a `char` data type, so use `int` and you'll be safe.

HMM...   Aren't you glad you learned about break? The program keeps getting a character at a time until the user presses Enter (which produces a newline \n escape sequence). break stops the loop.

The Newline Consideration

Although getchar() gets a single character, control isn't returned to your program until the user presses Enter. The getchar() function actually instructs C to accept input into a *buffer*, which is a memory area reserved for input. The buffer isn't released until the user presses Enter, and then the buffer's contents are released a character at a time. This means two things. One, the user can press the Backspace key to correct bad character input as long as he or she hasn't pressed Enter. Two, the Enter keypress is left on the input buffer if you don't get rid of it.

Getting rid of the Enter keypress is a problem that all beginning C programmers must face. There are several solutions, but none is extremely elegant. Consider the following segment of a program:

```
printf("What are your two initials?\n");
firstInit = getchar();
lastInit  = getchar();
```

You would think that if the user typed GT, the G would go in the variable firstInit and the T would go in lastInit, but that's not what happens. The first getchar() doesn't finish until the user presses Enter, because the G was going to the buffer. Only when the user presses Enter does the G leave the buffer and go to the program, but *then* the Enter is *still* on the buffer! Therefore, the second getchar() sends that Enter (actually, the \n that represents Enter) to lastInit! The T is still left for a subsequent getchar() (if there is one).

PSST! One way to fix this problem is to insert an extra `getchar()` that captures the Enter but doesn't do anything with it. That's why the Blackjack program in Appendix B has a `getchar()` on a line by itself—to capture the Enter and clear the buffer to make room for the next character input.

A Little Faster: getch()

A character input function named `getch()` helps eliminate the left-over Enter keypress that `getchar()` leaves. `getch()` is *unbuffered*—that is, `getch()` gets whatever keypress the user types immediately and doesn't wait for an Enter keypress. The drawback to `getch()` is that the user can't press the Backspace key to correct bad input. For example, with `getchar()`, a user could press Backspace if he or she typed a B instead of a D. The B would be taken off the buffer by the Backspace, and the D would be left for `getchar()` to get once Enter was pressed. Because `getch()` does *not* buffer input, there is no chance of pressing Backspace. The following code gets two characters without an Enter keypress following each one:

```
printf("What are your two initials?\n");
firstInit = getch();
lastInit  = getch();
```

`getch()` is a little faster than `getchar()` because it doesn't wait for an Enter keypress before grabbing the user's keystrokes and continuing. You therefore don't need a stand-alone `getch()` to get rid of the \n as you do with `getchar()`.

PSST! `getch()` does *not* echo the input characters to the screen as `getchar()` does. Therefore, you must follow `getch()` with a mirror-image `putch()` if you want the user to see on the screen the character he or she typed.

The next chapter explains more built-in functions, including two that quickly input and output strings as easily as this chapter's I/O functions work with characters.

Happy Landings

 Use `getchar()` and `putchar()` to input and output single characters.

 Use a stand-alone `getchar()` to get rid of the Enter keypress if you don't want to capture it. You also can create a loop to call `getchar()` *until* the return value is `\n`, as shown in the sample code.

 Use `getch()` to get *unbuffered* single characters as soon as the user types them.

Shot Down

 Don't use a character I/O function with character variables. Use an `int` variable instead.

 Don't forget to print character input using `putch()` if you want that input echoed on the screen as the user types.

In Review

This chapter's goal was to explain a few additional input and output functions. The functions presented here are character I/O functions. Unlike `scanf()` and `printf()`, the `getchar()`, `getch()`, `putchar()`, and `putch()` functions input and output single characters at a time.

You'll often find the `getch()` and `getchar()` functions used inside large input routines that build input. This means that these functions get a character at a time from the keyboard and add those characters to an array that is checked against a string value of some kind.

Code Example

```
printf("I'm going to print a report now.\n");
printf("Is your printer turned on (y/n)? ");
ans = getch();  /* Gets the user's answer */
if (ans == 'n')
   { printf("I'll wait. Press Enter when you have it
on...\n");
     ans = getch();  /* Waits for Enter keypress */
   }
/* The report printing code would follow */
```

Code Analysis

This code asks the user a yes-or-no question and waits for the user to respond with a y or an n. The if ensures that the message prints if the user enters n. If the user does not yet have the printer on, the program waits to give the user a chance to turn the printer on. (A report couldn't be printed otherwise.) The user lets the program know when the printer is turned on by pressing Enter.

Can You Tell Me More About Strings?

C's Built-In Character and String Functions

This chapter shows you ways to take work off your shoulders and put it on C's. C includes lots of helpful built-in functions in addition to ones like `strlen()`, `getchar()`, and `printf()` that you've read about so far.

Fun Fact
Your compiler might have other useful functions. Check its documentation.

There are many more built-in functions than there is room for in a single chapter. This chapter explains the most common and most helpful character and string functions. In the next chapter, you'll learn about some numeric functions.

Character-Testing Functions

There are several built-in *character-testing functions.* Now that you know how to use `getchar()` and `getch()` to get single characters, the character-testing functions can help you determine exactly what kind of input characters your program receives. You can set up `if` logic to execute certain courses of action based on the results of the character tests.

PSST!   You should include the `ctype.h` header file at the top of any program that uses the character functions described here.

The `isalpha()` function returns true (which is 1 to C) if the value in its parentheses is an alphabetic character a through z (or the upper-case A through Z) and returns false (which is 0 to C) if the value in parentheses is any other character. Consider this `if`:

```
if (isalpha(inChar))
    { printf("Your input was a letter.\n"); }
```

The message prints only if `inChar` contains an alphabetic letter.

C has a corresponding function named `isdigit()` that returns true if the parentheses value is a number from 0 through 9. The following `if` prints A number if `inChar` contains a digit:

```
if (isdigit(inChar))
   { printf("A number\n"); }
```

HMM... Do you see why these are called *character-testing* functions? Both `isalpha()` and `isdigit()` test character content and return the relational result of the test.

Is the Case Correct?

The `isupper()` and `islower()` functions let you know if a variable contains an uppercase or lowercase value. Using `isupper()` keeps you from having to write long `if` statements like this:

```
if ((inLetter >= 'A') && (inLetter <= 'Z'))
   { printf("Letter is uppercase\n"); }
```

Instead, use `isupper()` in place of the logical comparison:

```
if (isupper(inLetter))
   { printf("Letter is uppercase\n"); }
```

PSST! `islower()` tests for lowercase values in the same way as `isupper()` tests for uppercase values.

Case-Changing Functions

There are two important character-changing functions (also called *character-mapping functions*) that can change their arguments. Unlike `isupper()` and `islower()`, which only *test* character values, `toupper()`

and `tolower()` *change* variables to a different case. `toupper()` converts its parentheses argument to uppercase (if it is not uppercase already), and `tolower()` changes its parentheses argument to lowercase (if it is not already).

The following program segment prints `yes` or `no` to illustrate the `toupper()` function. Without `toupper()`, the `if` logical test would have to test for lowercase letters as well.

```
if (toupper(userInput) == 'Y')
    { printf("yes\n"); }
else
    { printf("no\n"); }
```

PSST! The Blackjack program uses `toupper()` in the `getAns()` function to return the uppercase version of whatever value the user types:

```
return toupper(ans);
```

String Functions

The `string.h` header file contains descriptions for more functions than just `strcpy()` and `strlen()`. This section explains the `strcat()` function that lets you merge two character arrays as long as they hold strings. `strcat()` stands for *string concatenation*.

`strcat()` takes one string and appends it to, or adds it onto the end of, another. Here is a code fragment that shows what happens with `strcat()`:

```
char first[25] = "Peter";
char last[25] = " Parker";
strcat(first, last);  /* Adds last to the end of first */
printf("I am %s\n", first);  /* Prints Peter Parker */
```

`strcat()` requires two string arguments. `strcat()` takes the second string and tacks it onto the end of the first one.

YIKES!

You are responsible for making sure that the first array is large enough to hold *both* strings.

HMM... Because the second argument for `strcat()` is not changed, you can use a string literal in place of a character array for the second argument if you like.

An easy way to print and get strings is provided by the `puts()` and `gets()` functions. Their descriptions are in `stdio.h`, so you don't have to add an additional header file for `puts()` and `gets()`. `puts()` sends a string to the screen, and `gets()` gets a string from the keyboard. The following program demonstrates `gets()` and `puts()`. As you look through it, notice that neither `printf()` nor `scanf()` is required to input and print strings.

```
#include <stdio.h>
#include <string.h>
main()
{
   char city[15];
   char st[3];  /* Leave 1 for null zero */
   char fullLocation[18] = "";  /* Put empty string here */
   puts("What town do you live in? ");
   gets(city);
   puts("What state do you live in? (2-letter abbreviation)");
   gets(st);
   /* Concatenates the strings */
   strcat(fullLocation, city);  /* Adds a comma and a space */
   strcat(fullLocation, ", ");  /* to end of city */
   strcat(fullLocation, st);  /* Adds the state
                                 to end of city */
```

```
    puts("\nYou live in ");
    puts(fullLocation);
    return 0;
}
```

PSST!   strcat() has to be used three times: once to add the city,
once for the comma, and once to tack the state onto the end
of the city.

Here is the output from a sample run of this program:

```
What town do you live in?
Jacksonville
What state do you live in? (2-letter abbreviation)
FL

You live in
Jacksonville, FL
```

PSST!   puts() automatically puts a newline at the end of every
string it prints. You don't have to add a \n at the end of an
output string unless you want an extra blank line printed.

Skip This, It's Technical

gets() converts the Enter keypress to a null
zero to ensure that the data obtained from the
keyboard winds up being a null-terminated string instead of an
array of single characters.

Happy Landings

 Use C's built-in character-testing and character-mapping functions so that your programs won't have to work as hard to determine the case of character data.

 Use `gets()` to get strings and `puts()` to print strings.

 Use `strcat()` to merge two strings.

Shot Down

 Don't concatenate two strings with `strcat()` unless you're positive that the first character array can hold the strings after they're merged.

 Don't put a newline inside the `puts()` string unless you want an extra line printed. `puts()` automatically adds a newline to the end of strings.

In Review

The goal of this chapter was to show you some built-in character and string functions that help you test and change strings. A string is a literal list of characters, explicitly stated inside quotation marks or stored in a character array. The string functions presented in this chapter work on both string literals and arrays.

There are functions that test characters for digits and letters, convert uppercase and lowercase characters to their opposites, concatenate (merge) strings, and allow for quick input and output of strings.

Code Example

```
printf("What is your name? ");
gets(name);
printf("Are you sure that %s is your name (y/n)? ", name);
ans = getch();
```

```
if (toupper(ans) == 'Y')
{  for (i = 0; i< = strlen(name); i++)
     { nameNew[i] = toupper(name[i]); }
   printf("Your name in uppercase letters is %s.\n", nameNew);
}
```

Code Analysis

This code first asks the user for his or her name. The name is entered
using a gets() function. If the user verifies that the name is entered
correctly, the for statement converts each character in the name to
an uppercase letter. The for loop steps through the array, sending
each character through the toupper() function and storing the
uppercase letters in an array named nameNew.

Can C Do My Math Homework?

The Built-In Numeric Functions Show You

This chapter extends your knowledge of built-in functions to the numeric functions. C helps you do math that the C operators can't do alone. More than anything else, the C built-in numeric functions supply routines that you don't have to write yourself.

A lot of C's built-in math functions are highly technical. Not that their use is difficult, but their purpose might be. Unless you need trigonometric and advanced math functions, you might not find a use for many of the functions described in this chapter.

  Some people program in C for years and never need many of these functions. You should read this chapter's material to get an idea of what C can accomplish so you'll know what's available if you ever do need these functions.

Practicing Your Math

All the functions this chapter describes require the use of the `math.h` header file. Be sure to include `math.h` along with `stdio.h` if you use a math function. The first few math functions are not so much math functions as they are numeric functions. These functions convert numbers to and from other numbers.

The `floor()` and `ceil()` functions are called the *floor* and *ceiling* functions, respectively. They "push down" and "push up" non-integers to their next lower or next higher integer value. For example, if you wanted to compute how many dollar bills are in a certain amount of change that includes dollars and cents, you could use `floor()` on the amount. The following code does just that:

```
change = amtPaid - cost;  /* Floating-point values */
dollars = floor(change);
printf("The change includes %f dollar bills.\n", dollars);
```

YIKES!

Although `ceil()` and `floor()` convert their arguments to integers, both functions return a `float` value! That's why the `dollars` variable was printed using the `%f` conversion code.

The `ceil()` function finds the next highest integer (which is the opposite of `floor()`). Both `ceil()` and `floor()` work with negative values too, as the following few lines show:

```
lowVal1 = floor(18.5);    /* Stores  18.0 */
lowVal2 = floor(-18.5);   /* Stores -19.0 */
hiVal1 = ceil(18.5);      /* Stores  19.0 */
hiVal2 = ceil(-18.5);     /* Stores -18.0 */
```

HMM... The negative values make sense when you think about the direction of negative numbers. The next integer *down* from –18.5 is –19, and the next integer *up* from –18.5 is –18.

HMM... See, these functions aren't so bad, and they come in handy when you need them.

Doing More Conversions

Two other numeric functions convert numbers to other values. The `fabs()` function returns the floating-point *absolute value*. When you first hear about absolute value, it sounds like something you'll never need. The absolute value of a number, whether it is negative or positive, is the positive version of the number. Both of these printf() functions print 25:

```
printf("Absolute value of 25.0 is %.0f.\n", fabs(25.0));
printf("Absolute value of -25.0 is %.0f.\n", fabs(-25.0));
```

 **HMM...** The floating-point answers print without decimal places because of the .0 inside the %f conversion codes.

 PSST! Absolute value is useful for computing differences in ages, weight, and distance. The difference between two people's ages is always a positive number, no matter how you subtract one from the other.

Two additional mathematical functions might come in handy even if you don't do heavy scientific and math programming. The pow() function raises a value to a power, and the sqrt() function returns the square root of a value.

 PSST! You can't compute the square root of a negative number. The fabs() function can help ensure that you don't try to take the square root of a negative number by converting the number to a positive value before you compute the square root.

YIKES!

If the preceding descriptions sound foreign, perhaps a picture will bring back fond high school algebra memories. Figure 20.1 shows the familiar math symbols used for pow() and sqrt().

Figure 20.1.

Looking at the math symbols for pow() and sqrt().

If a C programmer does this:	A mathematician does this:
x = pow(4, 6);	$x = 4^6$
x = sqrt(value);	$x = \sqrt{value}$

The following code prints the value of 10 raised to the third power and the square root of 64:

```
printf("10 raised to the 3rd power is %.0f.\n",
    pow(10.0, 3.0));
printf("The square root of 64 is %.0f.\n", sqrt(64.0));
```

Here is the output of these printf() functions:

```
10 raised to the 3rd power is 1000.
The square root of 64 is 8.
```

Getting into Trig and Other Really Hard Stuff

Only a handful of readers will need the trigonometric and logarithmic functions. If you know you won't, or if you hope you won't, go ahead and skip to the next section. Those of you who need them now don't require much explanation, so not much is given.

The primary trigonometric functions are explained in Table 20.1. They each require an argument expressed in radians.

Table 20.1. C's trigonometric functions.

Function	Description
cos(x)	Returns the cosine of the angle x.
sin(x)	Returns the sine of the angle x.
tan(x)	Returns the tangent of the angle x.

Skip This, It's Technical

If you want to supply an argument in degrees instead of in radians, you can convert from degrees to radians with this formula:

```
radians = degrees * (3.14159 / 180.0);
```

The primary log functions are shown in Table 20.2.

Table 20.2. C's logarithmic functions.

Function	Description
exp(x)	Returns e, the base of the natural logarithm, raised to a power specified by x (e^x).
log(x)	Returns the natural logarithm of the argument x, mathematically written as $\ln(x)$. x must be positive.
log10(x)	Returns the base-10 logarithm of the argument x, mathematically written as $\log10(x)$. x must be positive.

Getting Random

For games and simulation programs, you often need to generate random values. C's built-in `rand()` function does just that. It returns a random number from 0 to 32767. The `rand()` function requires the `stdlib.h` (*standard library*) header file. If you want to narrow the random numbers, you can use `%` to do so. The following expression puts a random number from 1 to 6 in the variable `dice`:

```
dice = (rand() % 5) + 1;  /* From 1 to 6 */
```

Skip This, It's Technical

Because a die can have a value from 1 to 6, the modulus operator returns the integer division remainder (0 through 5), and then a 1 is added to that to produce a die value.

There's one crazy thing you must do if you want a *truly* random value. It is described next.

HMM... You might always want a different set of random numbers produced each time a program runs. Games need such randomness. However, many simulations and scientific studies need to repeat the same set of random numbers. `rand()` will always do that if you don't *seed* the random-number generator.

To seed the random-number generator means to give it an initial base value from which the `rand()` function can offset with a random number. Use `srand()` to seed the random-number generator. The number inside `srand()`'s parentheses must be different every time you run the program unless you want to produce the same set of random values.

The trick to giving `srand()` a different number each run is to put the exact time of day inside `srand()`'s parentheses. Your computer keeps track of the time of day down to hundredths of a second.

Because there's no time to go into much detail, let's cut to the chase and see how most C programmers produce truly random values. The following code is similar to a section from the Blackjack game in Appendix B. The comments explain things that need explaining at this point.

```
time_t t;  /* Goes with your variable definitions
              such as int i;                       */
srand(time(&t));  /* Seeds with the time of day */
subDraw = (rand() % (numCards));  /* Ensures that a random
                                     card is drawn from a
                                     52-card deck          */
```

PSST!   You must include `time.h` before seeding the random-number generator with the time of day as done here.

HMM...   The bottom line is this: If you add the two weird-looking time statements shown here, `rand()` will always be random and will produce different results every time you run a program.

Happy Landings

    Use the built-in numeric functions when you can so that you won't have to write code to perform the same calculations.

Lots of the numeric functions such as `floor()`, `ceil()`, and `fabs()` convert one number to another.

 Be sure to seed the random-number generator with the time of day if you want random numbers with `rand()` to be different every time you run a program.

Shot Down

Don't feel that you must master the trig and log functions if you don't need them now. Many C programmers never use them.

Don't use an integer variable to hold the return value from this chapter's math functions (unless you typecast the function return values) because they return `floats` or `doubles` even though some, like `ceil()`, produce whole-number results.

In Review

The goal of this chapter was to explain lots of built-in math functions that can make numeric data processing easier. C contains a rich assortment of integer functions, numeric conversion functions, time and date functions, and random-number generating functions.

You don't have to understand every function in this chapter at this time. You might write hundreds of C programs and never use many of these functions. Nevertheless, they are in C if you need them.

Code Example

```
po2 = pow(2.0, 2.0);
printf("2 raised to the 2nd power is %.0f\n", po2);
s2 = sqrt(49);
printf("The square root of 49 is %.0f\n", s2);
si628 = sin(6.28);
printf("The sine of 6.28 is %f\n", si628);
r01 = rand();
printf("A random number from 0 to 1 is %f\n", r01);
```

Code Analysis

These code lines give quick examples of how you'd use some of the math functions described in this chapter. The program contains four pairs of statements. Each pair contains a function call and the output of that function call's resulting value.

Notice that `rand()` is the only function in the code that doesn't accept an argument. If the `rand()` function based its answer on a value you passed, `rand()` wouldn't be very random.

Part 4
C Programs and Lots of Data

Printers always seem to be
more efficient at 10,000 feet!

How Does C Work with Lists?

Using Arrays

The really nice thing about this chapter is that it covers absolutely nothing new. You've worked with arrays when you've stored strings in character arrays throughout this book. This chapter simply hones that concept of arrays and demonstrates that you can create an array of any data type, not just the `char` data type.

An array of characters is just a list of characters that has a name. Similarly, an array of integers is just a list of integers that has a name, and an array of floating-point values is just a list of floating-point values that has a name. Instead of referring to each of the array elements by a different name, you only have to refer to them by the array name and distinguish them with a subscript enclosed in brackets.

Reviewing Arrays

All arrays contain values called *elements*. An array can contain *only* elements that are of the same type. In other words, you can't have an array that has a floating-point value, a character value, and an integer value.

To define a regular variable, you only have to specify its data type next to the variable name:

```
int i;
```

To define an array, you must add brackets after the name and specify the maximum number of elements that you will ever store in the array:

```
int i[25];
```

If you want to initialize a character array with an initial string, you know that you can do this:

```
char name[6] = "Italy";   /* Leave room for the null! */
```

Skip This, It's Technical

Once you define an array to a certain size, don't try to store more elements than that original size. The `strcpy()` function will *let* you store a string longer than `Italy` in `name`, but the result would be disastrous because other data in memory could be overwritten unintentionally.

PSST! If the initial array needs to be larger than the initial value you assign, specify a larger array size:

```
char name[80] = "Italy";   /* Leaves lots of
                              extra room */
```

Doing this makes room for a string much longer than `Italy` if you want to store a longer string in `name`. For example, you might want to use `gets()` to get a string from the user that would easily be longer than `Italy`.

YIKES!

Don't make your arrays larger than you think you'll need. Arrays can consume a large amount of memory, and the more elements you reserve, the less memory you have for your program and the other variables.

You can initialize an array one element at a time when you define the array by enclosing the elements in braces and following the array name with an equals sign. For example, the following statement both defines an integer array *and* initializes it with five values:

```
int vals[5] = {10, 40, 70, 90, 120};
```

YIKES!

As a review, Figure 21.1 shows what `vals` looks like in memory. The numbers in brackets indicate subscripts. No null zero is at the end of the array because null zeros terminate only strings.

Figure 21.1.

After defining and initializing the vals array.

The vals array

10	vals[0]
40	vals[1]
70	vals[2]
90	vals[3]
120	vals[4]

The first subscript of all C arrays begins at 0.

The following statement defines and initializes two arrays—a floating-point array and a double floating-point array. Because C is free-form, you can continue the initialization list over more than one line.

```
float money[10] = {6.23, 2.45, 8.01, 2.97, 6.41};
double annualSal[6] = {43565.78, 75674.23, 90001.34,
                       10923.45, 39845.82};
```

You also can define and initialize a character array with individual characters:

```
char grades[5] = {'A', 'B', 'C', 'D', 'F'};
```

Because a null zero is not in the last element, grades consists of individual characters but not a string. If the last element were initialized with '\0', which represents the null zero, you could have treated grades as a string and printed it with puts(), or printf() and the %s conversion code.

YIKES!

Always specify the number of subscripts when you define an array! There is one exception to this rule, however: If you assign an initial value or set of values to the array *at the time you define the array*, you can leave the brackets empty:

```
int ages[5] = {5, 27, 40, 65, 92};  /* Correct */
int ages[];  /* Incorrect */
int ages[] = {5, 27, 40, 65, 92};  /* Correct */
```

 HMM... sizeof() returns the number of bytes you *reserved* for the array, *not* the number of elements in which you have stored a value.

PSST! If you want to zero-out every element of an array, you can do so with a shortcut that C provides:

```
float amounts[100] = {0.0};  /* Zeroes-out all of
                                the array */
```

If you don't initialize an array, C won't either. Until you put values into an array, you have no idea exactly what's in the array.

Putting Values in Arrays

You don't always know the contents of an array at the time you define it. Often, array values come from a disk file, calculations, or from user input. Character arrays are easy to fill with strings because C supplies the `strcpy()` function. You can fill other types of arrays only a single element at a time. There is no shortcut function such as `strcpy()` that puts lots of integers or floating-point values in an array.

The following code defines an array of integers and asks the user for values that are stored in that array. Array elements, unlike regular variables that all have different names, are easy to work with because you can use a loop to count the subscripts, as done here:

```
int ages[3];
for (i = 0; i < 3; i++)
   { printf("What is the age of child #%d? ", i);
     scanf(" %d", &ages[i]);  /* Gets next age from user */
   }
```

PSST! The `initCardsScreen()` function in the Blackjack program in Appendix B uses a conditional operator to produce various numeric values that represent cards in the deck:

```
val = (val == 14) ? 1 : val; /* If val is 14,
                                reset to 1 */
```

We're Not Done Yet

This chapter explained the purpose of arrays. The next chapter explains exactly how to sort arrays in the order you want them and how to search arrays for a specific value.

Happy Landings

 Use arrays to hold lists of values of the same data type.

 Refer to the individual elements of an array with a subscript.

 Write `for` loops if you want to "step through" every array element, whether it be to initialize, print, or change the array elements.

Shot Down

 Don't try to use more elements in an array than you have defined subscripts.

 Don't use an array until you have initialized it with values.

In Review

The goal of this chapter was to teach you how to store data in lists called *arrays*. An array is nothing more than a bunch of variables. Each variable has the same name (the array name). You distinguish between the variables in the array (the array *elements*) by a numeric *subscript*. The first array element has a subscript of 0 and the rest count up from there.

Arrays are characterized by brackets that follow the array names. The array subscripts go inside the brackets when you need to refer to an individual array element.

Code Example

```
int i;
float grades[10];   /* Creates the array */
float avg = 0;
for (i = 0; i < 10; i++)
```

```
  { printf("What is student number %d's grade? ", i);
    scanf(" %f", &grades[i]);  /* Gets each grade
                                   from teacher */
    avg += grades[i]; }  /* Adds to total scores */
avg /= 10;  /* Computes average */
printf("\nThe average of all grades is %.2f.\n", avg);
```

Code Analysis

This code first creates work variables that hold an integer counter for the `for` loop, the `grades` array that will hold 10 grades, and the floating-point variable `avg` that will hold the average of those grades.

The program then asks the teacher for each of the 10 students' grades in the `for` loop. The last statement in the loop adds each grade to a running total of the grades. The total variable, named `avg`, is finally divided by 10 at the end of the program to hold the average of the grades.

How Can I Arrange and Alphabetize?

The Bubble Sort Does the Trick

 Putting your house in order: sorting   198

This chapter is a little different from a lot of the others. Instead of teaching you new C features, this chapter demonstrates the use of C language elements you've been learning throughout this book. This chapter focuses on arrays. You will see an application of the array concepts you learned in Chapter 21. This chapter strengthens your array understanding, and the next chapter explains a C alternative to arrays that sometimes comes in handy.

Putting Your House in Order: Sorting

Sorting is the computer term given to ordering lists of values. If you want to alphabetize a list of letters or names, or put a list of sales values into ascending order (*ascending* means from low to high and *descending* means from high to low), you will want to use a sorting routine. Of course, the list of values that you sort will be stored in an array because array values are so easily rearranged by their subscripts.

Think about how you'd put a deck of cards in order if you threw them up in the air and let them fall. You would pick them up, one by one, looking at how the current card fit in with the others in your hand. Often you would rearrange some that you already held. The same type of process is done for sorting an array; often you have to rearrange values that are in the array.

There are several computer methods for sorting values. This chapter teaches you about the *bubble sort*. The bubble sort isn't extremely efficient compared to other sorts, but it's the easiest to understand. The name *bubble sort* comes from the nature of the sort. During a sort, the lower values "float" up the list each time a pass is made through the data. Figure 22.1 shows the process of sorting five numbers using a bubble sort.

Figure 22.1.

*During each pass,
the lower values
"float" to the top
of the array.*

Before sorting: 50
    32
    93
     2
    74

During first pass, C compares the first value
to the second. Because 32 is less than 50, they
switch places: 32
    50
    93
     2
    74

It then compares 32 and 93 and leaves them
where they are. Next, C compares 32 and 2. Because
2 is the lesser value, 32 and 2 switch places:
     2
    50
    93
    32
    74

Finally, it compares 2, the new first value in
the list, to 74 and leaves them.

After first pass: 2
    50
    93
    32
    74

During second pass, C compares the second value, 50,
to 93 and leaves them. It then compares 50 to 32 and
switches them: 2
    32
    93
    50
    74

C then compares the second value, 32, to 74 and
leaves them.

After second pass: 2
    32
    93
    50
    74

This process continues until all the numbers
have been sorted.

After third pass: 2
    32
    50
    93
    74

After fourth pass: 2
    32
    50
    74
    93   (sorted)

Fun Fact
Other sorting methods include the QuickSort, the Combsort, the Heapsort, and the Shell-Metzner method.

The next program sorts a list of 10 numbers. The numbers are randomly generated using `rand()`. The bubble sort routine is little more than a nested `for` loop. The inner loop walks through the list, swapping any pair of values that is out of order down the list. The outer loop causes the inner loop to run several times (one time for each item in the list). An added bonus that is common to many improved bubble sort routines is the testing to see if a swap took place during any iteration of the inner loop. If no swap took place, the outer loop finishes early (via a `break` statement). Therefore, if the loop is sorted to begin with, or if only a few passes are needed to sort the list, the outer loop doesn't have to finish all its planned repetitions.

YIKES!

Yes, this program is long. However, most of this book has shown you small samples of code. It would be a good idea to step through this program and figure out what it's doing. Use a pencil and paper to jot down variable values.

```c
#include <stdio.h>
#include <stdlib.h>
/* Program that sorts a list of 10 numbers */
main()
{  int cnt, inner, outer, didSwap, temp;
   int nums[10];  /* Will hold the 10 numbers */
   /* Fills an array with random numbers from 1 to 100 */
   for (cnt = 0; cnt < 10; cnt++)
      { nums[cnt] = (rand() % 99) + 1; }
   /* Prints the list before it is sorted */
   puts("\nHere is the list before the sort:");
   for (cnt = 0; cnt < 10; cnt++)
      { printf("%d\n", nums[cnt]); }
   /* Sorts the array */
   for (outer = 0; outer < 9; outer++)
      { didSwap = 0;  /* Becomes 1 (true) if list
                         is not yet ordered */
      for (inner = outer; inner < 10; inner++)
         { if (nums[inner] < nums[outer])
```

```
         {  temp = nums[inner];
            nums[inner] = nums[outer];
            nums[outer] = temp;
            didSwap = 1;   /* True because a swap
                                   took place */
         }
      }
   if (didSwap == 0)  /* Quits if list is now sorted */
      { break; }
   }
   /* Prints the list after it is sorted */
   printf("\nHere is the list after the sort:\n");
   for (cnt = 0; cnt < 10; cnt++)
      { printf("%d\n", nums[cnt]); }
   return 0;
}
```

The output from this sorting program is as follows:

```
Here is the list before the sort:
 71
 54
 58
 29
 31
 78
 2
 77
 82
 71

Here is the list after the sort:
 2
 29
 31
 54
 58
 71
 71
 77
 78
 82
```

PSST! Your output might be different because `rand()` produces different results each time the program runs.

The swapping of the variables inside the inner loop is as follows:

```
temp = nums[inner];
nums[inner] = nums[outer];
nums[outer] = temp;
```

You might wonder why an extra variable, `temp`, was needed to swap two variables' values. A natural (and incorrect) tendency when swapping two variables might be this:

```
nums[inner] = nums[outer];   /* Does NOT swap the */
nums[outer] = nums[inner];   /* two values        */
```

The first assignment wipes out the value of `nums[inner]` so that the second assignment has nothing to assign. Therefore, a third variable is required to swap any two variables.

PSST! If you wanted to sort the list in descending order, you would only have to change the less-than sign to a greater-than sign right before the swapping code:

```
/* Top of program would go here */
{ if (nums[inner] > nums[outer])
    /* Rest of program follows */
```

HMM... If you wanted to alphabetize a list of characters, you could do so by testing and swapping character array values just as you've done here. In Chapter 24 you will learn how to sort lists of string data.

Happy Landings

 Use an ascending sort when you want to arrange array values from low to high.

 Use a descending sort when you want to arrange array values from high to low.

The nested `for` loop, such as the one you saw in this chapter, is a perfect statement to produce a bubble sort.

Shot Down

Don't try to swap the values of two variables unless you introduce a third work variable to hold the in-between value.

Sorting routines don't have to be hard. Start with the one listed in this chapter and adapt it to your own needs.

In Review

The goal of this chapter was to familiarize you with the bubble sort method of ordering and alphabetizing values in arrays. You don't need any new C commands to sort values. Sorting is one of the primary array advantages. It shows that arrays are a better storage method than separately named variables. The array subscripts let you step through the array and swap values when needed to sort the array.

Code Example

```
/* Sorts the array backwards (in descending order) */
for (outer = 0; outer < 9; outer++)
   { didSwap = 0;  /* Becomes 1 (true) if list
                      is not yet ordered */
     for (inner = outer; inner < 10; inner++)
       {  if (nums[inner] > nums[outer])  /* Descending
                                             test */
```

```
          {  temp = nums[inner];  /* Swaps if needed */
             nums[inner] = nums[outer];
             nums[outer] = temp;
             didSwap = 1;   /* True because a swap
                               took place */
          }
       }
    if (didSwap == 0)  /* Quits if list is now sorted */
      { break; }
  }
```

Code Analysis

This section of code forms the complete descending sort code
needed to sort this chapter's list of 10 random numbers backwards.
The only difference between a descending sort and an ascending
sort is the `if` comparison at the top of the swapping code.

This `if` statement is marked by the comment /* `Descending test` */.
The nested loops test pairs of numbers in the list. If the lowest value
in the pair of numbers is greater than the second value in the pair,
the swap code executes to reverse the two values. (The swapping
code consists of the four lines marked by the /* `Swaps if needed` */
comment.)

What's the Point?

Using Pointers, You'll Find Out

Pointer variables, often called just pointers, let you do much more with C than you can with programming languages that don't support pointers. When you first learn about pointers, you'll probably ask, "What's the big deal?" (Even after you master them, you still might ask the same thing!) Actually, pointers provide the means for the true power of C programming. This book exposes the tip of the pointer iceberg. The concepts you learn here will form the foundation of your C programming future.

Memory Addresses

Inside your computer is a bunch of memory. The memory holds your program as it executes and also your program's variables. Every memory location has a different address, just as every house has a different address. Not coincidentally, the memory locations have their own *addresses* as well. As with house addresses, the memory addresses are all unique; no two are the same.

Figure 23.1 shows you the look of the computer's memory. The address has nothing to do with the data stored in that address. All computer addresses begin at zero and increment from there.

When you define variables, C finds an unused place in memory and attaches a name to that memory location. That's a good thing. Instead of having to remember that an order number is stored at memory address 34532, you only have to remember the name orderNum. The name orderNum is *much* easier to remember than a number.

PSST!   The support of variable names is just one of many programming shortcuts that compilers provide.

Figure 23.1.

The computer contains lots of memory, and each memory location has a unique address.

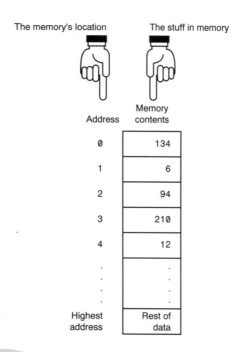

The memory's location   The stuff in memory

Address   Memory contents

Address	Memory contents
0	134
1	6
2	94
3	210
4	12
.	.
.	.
.	.
Highest address	Rest of data

Skip This, It's Technical

Figure 23.1 is somewhat misleading. PC addresses are often *segmented* into *segments* and *offsets*. The PC's memory is divided into segments that represent sections of memory in the same way that chapters in a book represent sections of the book. The offset is a second number added to the segment's address to get to a particular memory location. Someday we'll be programming computers that use a strict *flat memory model*, which is a fancy way of saying we'll be able to throw that segment stuff out the door and get back to the basics of giving every memory location a sequential address starting at 0 and continuing until the memory runs out.

Defining Pointer Variables

As with any other type of variable, you must define a pointer variable before you can use it. Before going further, you need to learn two new operators. Table 23.1 shows them along with their descriptions.

Table 23.1. The pointer operators.

Operator	Description
&	Address-of operator
*	Dereferencing operator

YIKES!

You've seen the * before. How does C know the difference between multiplication and dereferencing? The context of how you use them determines how C interprets them. You've also seen the & before `scanf()` variables. The & in `scanf()` is the address-of operator. `scanf()` requires that you send it the address of non-array variables.

The following is how you'd define an integer and a floating-point variable:

```
int num;
float value;
```

To define an integer pointer variable and a floating-point pointer variable, you simply insert an *:

```
int * pNum;   /* Defines two pointer variables */
float * pValue;
```

There's nothing special about the names of pointer variables. Lots of C programmers like to preface pointer variable names with a p as done here, but you can name them anything you like.

PSST! All data types have corresponding pointer data types. There are character pointers, long integer pointers, and so on.

Pointer variables hold addresses of other variables. That's their primary purpose. Use the address-of operator, &, to assign the address of one variable to a pointer. Until you assign an address of a variable to a pointer, the pointer is uninitialized and you can't use it for anything.

The following code defines an integer variable named age and initializes it to 19. Then a pointer named pAge is defined and initialized to point to age. The address-of operator reads just like it sounds. The second line that follows tells C to put the address of age into pAge.

```
int age = 19;        /* Stores a 19 in age */
int * pAge = &age;   /* Links up the pointer */
```

You have no idea exactly what address C will store age at. However, whatever address C uses, pAge will hold that address. When a pointer variable holds the address of another variable, it in effect *points* to that variable. Assuming that age is stored at the address 18826 (only C knows exactly where it is stored), Figure 23.2 shows what the resulting memory would look like.

Figure 23.2.

The variable pAge points to age if pAge holds the address of age.

Address	Memory	Variable name
.	.	
.	.	
.	.	
18826	19	age
.	.	
.	.	
.	.	
20886	18826	pAge

HMM... Just because you define two variables back-to-back doesn't mean that C stores them back-to-back in memory. C *might* store them together, but it also might not.

YIKES!

Never try to set the address of one type of variable to a pointer variable of a different type. C will only let you assign the address of one type of variable to a pointer defined with the same data type.

The * isn't part of a pointer variable's name. You will use the * *dereferencing operator* for several things, but in the pointer definition, the * exists only to tell C that the variable is a pointer and not a regular variable. The following four statements do *exactly the same thing* as the previous two statements. Notice that you don't use * to store the address of a variable into a pointer variable unless you are also defining the pointer at the same time.

```
int age;      /* Defines a regular integer */
int * pAge;   /* Defines a pointer to an integer */
age = 19;     /* Stores 19 in age */
pAge = &age;  /* Links up the pointer */
```

Using the Dereferencing *

As soon as you link up a pointer to another variable, you can work with the other value by *dereferencing* the pointer. Programmers never use an easy word when a hard one will do just as well and confuse more people. Dereferencing just means to use the pointer to get to the other variable. When you dereference, use the * dereferencing operator.

In a nutshell, here are two ways to change the value of age (assuming the variables are defined as described earlier):

```
age = 25;
```

and

```
*pAge = 25;  /* Stores 25 where pAge points */
```

Notice that you can use a variable name to store a value or dereference a pointer that points to the variable. You also can use a variable's value in the same way. Here are two ways to print the contents of age:

```
printf("The age is %d.\n", age);
```

and

```
printf("The age is %d.\n", *pAge);
```

The dereferencing operator is used when a function works with a pointer variable that it is sent. In Chapter 29, you'll learn how to pass pointers to functions. When a function uses a pointer variable that it is sent from another function, you must use the dereferencing operator before the variable name everywhere it appears. The

Blackjack program in Appendix B does this in the dealCard() function. The following lines from the function show the dereferencing operator being used:

```
subDraw = (rand() % (*numCards));  /* From 0 to numcards */
   cardDrawn = cards[subDraw];
   cards[subDraw] = cards[*numCards - 1];  /* Puts top
                                               card in */
```

Happy Landings

 Get comfortable with memory addresses because they form the basis of pointer usage.

 Use the & to produce the address of a variable.

 Use the * to define a pointer variable and to dereference a pointer variable. *pAge and age reference the same memory location as long as you've made pAge point to age.

Shot Down

 Don't try to make a pointer variable of one data type point to a variable of a different data type.

 Don't worry about the *exact* address that C uses for variable storage. If you use &, C will take care of the rest.

 Don't forget to use * when dereferencing your pointer, or you'll get the wrong value.

In Review

The goal of this chapter was to introduce you to pointer variables. A pointer variable is nothing more than a variable that holds the location of another variable. You can refer to the pointed-to variable by its name or by dereferencing the pointer.

Pointers have many uses in C, especially in advanced C programming. As you'll learn in the next chapter, arrays are nothing more than pointers in disguise. Because pointers offer more flexibility than arrays, most C programmers stop using arrays once they master pointers.

Code Example

```
char initial = 'G';  /* Defines a character variable */
char * pInitial;  /* Defines a character pointer variable */
float score = 97.4;  /* Defines a floating-point variable */
float * pScore;  /* Defines a floating-point
                    pointer variable */
pInitial = & initial;  /* Links the pointer to the data */
pScore = &score;
printf("The initial is %c.\n", *pInitial);
*pScore = 85.0;  /* Changes score, not pScore! */
```

Code Analysis

The code initializes two nonpointer variables—a character variable named initial and a floating-point variable named score. The code also defines two pointer variables and makes those pointer variables point to the regular variables.

As you can see in the last two statements, you can use a pointer variable to get to the contents of other variables. The printf() does not print the value of pInitial; rather, printf() prints the value of initial. The score variable, not pScore, is changed to 85.0 as well because of the dereferencing of the pointer.

How Are Arrays and Pointers Different?

They're the Same Thing in C

This chapter teaches how C's array and pointer variables share a lot of principles. As a matter of fact, an array is a special kind of pointer. Because of their similarities, you can use pointer notation to get to array values, and you can use array notation to get to pointed-at values.

Perhaps the most important reason to learn how arrays and pointers overlap is for character-string handling. By combining pointer notation (using the dereferencing operation) and array notation (using subscripts), you can store lists of character strings and reference them as easily as you reference array values of other data types.

Array Names Are Pointers

An array name is nothing more than a pointer to the first element in that array. The array name is not a pointer *variable,* though. Array names are known as *pointer constants.* The following statement defines an integer array and initializes it:

```
int vals[5] = {10, 20, 30, 40, 50};
```

You can reference the array by subscript notation. That much you know already. However, C does more than just attach subscripts to the values in memory. C sets up a pointer to the array and names that point to vals. You can never change the contents of vals. vals is like a fixed pointer variable whose address is locked in by C. Figure 24.1 shows you what C really does when you define and initialize vals.

Because the array name is a pointer (that can't be changed), you can print the first value in the array like this:

```
printf("The first value is %d.\n", vals[0]);
```

But more importantly for this chapter, you can print the first array value like this too:

```
printf("The first value is %d.\n", *vals);
```

Figure 24.1.

*The array name is
a pointer to the
first value in the
array.*

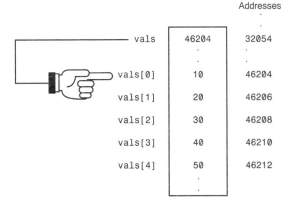

Getting Down in the List

Because an array name is nothing more than a pointer to the *first*
value in the array, if you want the second value, you only have to
add 1 to the array name and dereference *that* location. This set of
printf() lines:

```
printf("The first array value is %d.\n", vals[0]);
printf("The second array value is %d.\n", vals[1]);
printf("The third array value is %d.\n", vals[2]);
printf("The fourth array value is %d.\n", vals[3]);
printf("The fifth array value is %d.\n", vals[4]);
```

> **Skip This, It's Technical**
>
> The fact that an array is a fixed constant
> pointer is why you can't put an array name
> on the left side of an equals sign. You can't change a constant.
> (Remember, though, that C relaxes this rule only when you first
> define the array because C has yet to fix the array
> at a specific address.)

does *exactly* the same as these:

```
printf("The first array value is %d.\n", *(vals + 0));
printf("The second array value is %d.\n", *(vals + 1));
printf("The third array value is %d.\n", *(vals + 2));
printf("The fourth array value is %d.\n", *(vals + 3));
printf("The fifth array value is %d.\n", *(vals + 4));
```

YIKES!

If you're wondering about the importance of all this mess, hang tight. In a moment you'll see how C's pointer notation lets you make C act *almost* as if it has string variables.

Skip This, It's Technical

As you might remember, integers usually take more than 1 byte of memory storage. The preceding `printf()`s look as though they add 1 to the address inside `vals` to get to the next dereferenced memory location, but C helps you out here. C adds one *int size* when you add 1 to an `int` pointer (and one `double` size when you add 1 to a `double` pointer, and so on). The expression `*(vals + 2)` tells C that you want the *third integer* in the list that `vals` points to.

Characters and Pointers

The following two statements set up almost the same thing in memory. The only difference is that in the second statement, `pName` is a pointer *variable*, not a pointer constant:

're the Same Thing in C   219

```
char name[] = "Andrew B. Mayfair";   /* name points to A */
char * pName = "Andrew B. Mayfair";   /* pName points to A */
```

Because pName is a pointer variable, you *can* put it on the left side of
an equals sign! Therefore, you don't always have to use strcpy() if
you want to assign a character pointer a new string value. The
character pointer will only point to the first character in the string,
but %s and all the string functions work with character pointers just
as easily as with character arrays (since the two are the same thing)
because these functions know to stop at the null zero.

To put a different name in the name array, you have to use strcpy()
or assign the string one character at a time, but to make pName point
to a different name, you get to do this:

```
pName = "Theodore M. Brooks";
```

Skip This, It's Technical

The only reason string assignment works is
that C puts all your program's string literals
into memory somewhere and then *replaces* them in your program
with their addresses. C is not really putting Theodore M. Brooks into
pName because pName can hold only addresses. C is putting the
address of Theodore M. Brooks into pName.

HMM...   *Yea!* You now have a way to assign strings new values
without using strcpy(). It took a little work to get here,
but aren't you glad you made it? If so, settle down,
because there is just one catch (isn't there always?)

Be Careful with Lengths

It's okay to store string literals in character arrays as just described. The new strings can be shorter or longer than the previous string. That's nice, because you might recall that you can't store into a character array a string that is longer than the array you reserved initially.

You must be extremely careful, however, *not* to let the *program* store strings longer than the first string you point to with the character pointer. This is a little complex, but keep following along because this chapter stays as simple and short as possible. Never set up a character pointer variable like this:

```
main()
{
   char * name = "Tom Roberts";
/* Rest of program follows */
```

and then later let the user enter a new string with `gets()` like this:

```
gets(name);   /* Not very safe */
```

The problem with this statement is that the user might enter a string longer than `Tom Roberts`, the first string assigned to the character pointer. Although a character pointer can point to strings of any length, the `gets()` function, along with `scanf()`, `strcpy()`, and `strcat()`, doesn't know that it's being sent a character pointer. Because they might be sent a character array that can't change location, these functions map the newly created string directly over the location of the string in `name`. If a string longer than `name` is entered, other data areas could be overwritten.

YIKES!

Yes, this is a little tedious. You might have to read this section again later after you get more comfortable with pointers and arrays.

If you want to have the advantage of a character pointer—that is, if you want to be able to assign string literals to the pointer and still have the safety of arrays so that you can use the character pointer to get user input—you can do so with a little trick.

If you want to store user input in a string pointed to by a pointer, first reserve enough storage for that input string. The easiest way to do this is to reserve a character array, then assign a character pointer to the beginning element of that array:

```
char input[81];  /* Holds a string as long as
                      80 characters */
char *iptr = input;  /* Also could have done this:
                          char *iptr = &input[0]; */
```

Now you can input a string by using the pointer:

```
gets(iptr);  /* Makes sure that iptr points to
                the string typed by the user */
```

You also can assign the pointer string literals as long as those literals don't go beyond 81 bytes including the null zero.

Arrays of Pointers

If you want to use a bunch of pointers, create an array of them. An array of pointers is just as easy to define as an array of any other kind of data, except that you must include the * operator after the data type name. The following statements reserve an array of 25 integer pointers and an array of 25 character pointers:

```
int * ipara[25];   /* 25 pointers to integers */
char * cpara[25];  /* 25 pointers to characters */
```

The array of characters is most interesting because you can store a list of strings in the array. More accurately, you can *point* to various strings. The following program illustrates two things—how to initialize an array of strings at definition time and how to print them using a for loop:

```
#include <stdio.h>
main()
{
   int i;
   char * names[5] = {"Joe Swadley", "Richard Wikert",
                      "Keith Miller", "Dean Davenport",
                      "Stacy Riquet"};
   for (i = 0; i < 5; i++)
      { printf("Name %d: %s\n", i, names[i]); }
   return 0;
}
```

Happy Landings

 Use character pointers if you want to assign string literals directly.

Use either array subscript notation or pointer dereferencing to access array and pointer values.

Take a break. This was a lot of material!

Shot Down

Don't use a built-in function to fill a character pointer's location unless that character pointer was originally set up to point to a long string.

In Review

The goal of this chapter was to get you thinking about the similarities between arrays and pointers. An array name is really just a pointer that points to the first element in the array. Unlike pointer variables, an array name can't change. This is the primary reason an array name can't appear on the left side of an equals sign.

Using pointers allows more flexibility than arrays. You can directly assign a string literal to a character pointer variable, whereas you must use the `strcpy()` function to assign strings to arrays. You'll see many uses for pointer variables throughout your C programming career.

Code Example

```
char * days[7];
days[0] = "Sunday";
days[1] = "Monday";
days[2] = "Tuesday";
days[3] = "Wednesday";
days[4] = "Thursday";
days[5] = "Friday";
days[6] = "Saturday";
printf("Enter a number from 1 to 7: ");
scanf(" %d", &dayNum);
if (dayNum >= 1 || dayNum <= 7)
   { printf("That day is %s\n", days[dayNum - 1]); }
else
   { printf("You didn't enter a good number.\n"); }
```

Code Analysis

The array of seven pointer variables is created and then assigned to the seven days of the week string literals. The strings could have been assigned at the time `days` was defined, but this code assigns each string one at a time just to show you how it can be done.

The program then asks for a number. If the user enters a number from 1 to 7, the matching day element is printed. Because array elements begin at 0, 1 has to be subtracted from the user's number to match a day of the week name.

How Do I Store Lots of Data?

With Structures

Arrays and pointers are nice for lists of values, but those values must all be of the same data type. There will be times when you have different data types that must go together and be treated as a whole.

A perfect example would be a customer record. For each customer, you'd have to track a name (character array), balance (double floating-point), address (character array), city (character array), state (character array), and zip code (character array or long integer). Although you would want to be able to initialize and print individual items within the customer record, you'd also want to access the customer record as a whole, such as when you would write it to a customer disk file (which is explained in the next chapter).

The C *structure* is the vehicle by which you group data such as would appear in a customer record, and yet get to all the individual parts, called *members*. If you have many occurrences of that data and many customers, you would need an array of structures.

HMM...   Other languages have equivalent data groupings called *records*. The designers of C wanted to call them *structures*, however, so that's what they are in C.

Defining a Structure

The first thing you must do is tell C exactly what your structure will look like. When you define variables of built-in data types such as ints, you don't have to tell C what an int is because it already knows. When you want to define a structure, however, you must first tell C exactly what your structure looks like, and then you can define variables for that structure.

YIKES!

Try to view a structure as just a group of individual data types. The entire structure has a name and can be considered a single value taken as a whole (like a customer). The individual members of the structure are built-in data types, such as `int` and `char` arrays, that could represent an age and a name. You can access the individual members if you want to.

PSST!   A structure is a lot like a paper form with blanks. A blank form, such as one you might fill out when applying for a credit card, is useless by itself. If the credit card company prints 10,000 forms, that doesn't mean they have 10,000 customers. Only when someone fills out the form is there a customer, and only when you define a variable for the structure you describe will C give memory space to a structure variable.

To define an `int` variable, you only have to do this:

```
int i;
```

To define a structure variable, you must first define what the structure looks like, and *then* you can define a variable. One way to think of structures is to relate them to a Rolodex™ card file. Any data that might fit in a card file—such as an inventory, customer list, holiday gift list, recipe collection, and so on—makes a good candidate for a structure. All of these kinds of data would fit nicely in a Rolodex™ card filing system where each card has the same basic format but different data.

The `struct` statement defines the look (or layout) of a structure. Here is the format of `struct`:

```
struct [structure tag] {
    member definition;
    member definition;
        :
    member definition;
};
```

Again, the `struct` defines only the layout of a structure. The *structure tag* is a name you give to that particular structure's look, but the *structure tag* has nothing to do with a structure variable name you might create later. After you define the format of a structure, you can define variables.

The *member definitions* are nothing more than regular built-in data type definitions. Instead of defining variables, though, you are defining *members,* in effect giving a name to that particular part of the structure.

Skip This, It's Technical

You *can* define a variable at the same time as the `struct` declaration statement, but most C programmers don't do so. If you want to define a variable for the structure at the same time you declare the structure format itself, insert one or more variable names before the `struct` statement's closing semicolon.

YIKES!

This a lot to absorb. The example that follows will aid your understanding.

Let's say you're writing a program to track a simple retail computer inventory. You need to track a computer manufacturer, model, amount of disk space (in megabytes), amount of memory space (in megabytes), quantity, cost, and retail price.

First you must use `struct` to define a structure. Here is a good candidate:

```
struct invStruct {
   char manuf[25];   /* Manufacturer name */
   char model[15];   /* Model code */
   int  diskSpace;   /* Disk space in megabytes */
   int  memSpace;    /* Memory space in megabytes */
   int  quantity;    /* Number in the inventory */
   float cost;       /* Cost of computer */
   float price;      /* Retail price of computer */
};
```

Figure 25.1 shows you what this structure format looks like.

Figure 25.1.

The format of the invStruct *structure.*

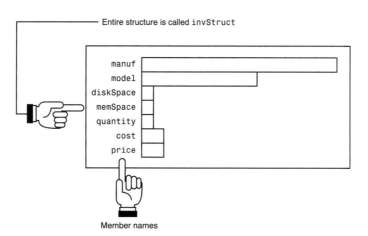

If you create a structure that you might use again sometime, consider putting it in its own header file, or in a header file along with other common structures. Use #include to pull that header file into any source code that needs it. If you ever need to change the structure definition, you have to look in only one place to change it—in its header file.

PSST!   That tip alone is worth the price of this book!

Often, a programmer puts structure declarations, like the following
one for invStruct, before main() and then defines variables for that
structure in main() and in any other functions below main(). To
create variables for the structure, you must do the same thing you
do when you create variables for any data type: Put the structure
name before a variable list. Because there is no data type named
invStruct, you must tell C that invStruct is a struct name. You
can define three structure variables like this:

```
#include "c:\\inv.h"  /* Includes the structure definition */
main()
{
   struct invStruct item1, item2, item3;
   /* Rest of program would follow */
```

You can insert whatever disk drive and path are needed before an
included filename as long as you put the drive and path inside
quotes before the filename, as with c:\\ here. Because a backslash
indicates that a control character (such as \n) might follow, you
must specify \\ if you want a resulting single backslash.

Now there are three variables into which you can put data. If you
wanted to define 500 structure variables, you would use an array:

```
main()
{
   struct invStruct items[500];
   /* Rest of program would follow */
```

Putting Data in Structure Variables

A new operator, the *dot operator*, lets you put data in the individual
members. Here is the format of the dot operator:

structureVariableName.memberName

To the left of the dot is always the name of a structure variable, such as item1 or employee[16]. To the right of the dot operator is always the name of a member from that structure, such as quantity, cost, or name.

The following program defines an array of three structure variables using the invStruct structure tag shown earlier. (The structure is assumed to be stored in inv.h to keep the example short.) The user is asked to fill the structure variables, and then the program prints them. In the next couple of chapters, you'll see how to output the structure variables to a disk file for long-term storage.

```c
/* First, include the file with the structure declaration */
#include "c:\\inv.h"
#include <stdio.h>
main()
{  int ctr;
   struct invStruct items[3];   /* Array of three
                                     structure variables */
   for (ctr = 0; ctr < 3; ctr++)
   {  printf("What is the manufacturer of item #%d? ",
          (ctr + 1));
      gets(items[ctr].manuf);
      puts("What is the model? ");
      gets(items[ctr].model);
      puts("How many megabytes of disk space? ");
      scanf(" %d", &items[ctr].diskSpace);
      puts("How many megabytes of memory space? ");
      scanf(" %d", &items[ctr].memSpace);
      puts("How many are there? ");
      scanf(" %d", &items[ctr].quantity);
      puts("How much does the item cost? ");
      scanf(" %f", &items[ctr].cost);
      puts("How much does the item retail for? ");
      scanf(" %f", &items[ctr].price);
      getchar();   /* Clears input of last newline
                       pressed for next round of input */
   }  /* Now, prints the data */
   printf("\n\nHere is the inventory: \n");
   for (ctr = 0; ctr < 3; ctr++)
   {  printf("#%d: Manufacturer: %s", (ctr + 1),
          items[ctr].manuf);
      printf("\nModel: %s", items[ctr].model);
      printf("\nDisk: %d megabytes\t", items[ctr].diskSpace);
      printf("Memory: %d megabytes\t", items[ctr].memSpace);
```

```
      printf("Quantity: %d units\n", items[ctr].quantity);
      printf("Cost: $%.2f\t", items[ctr].cost);
      printf("Selling price: $%.2f\n\n", items[ctr].price);
   }
   return 0;
}
```

Happy Landings

 Define structures when you want to group items of different data types.

 Declare a structure before defining a structure variable.

 Use the dot operator to access individual data members.

Shot Down

 Don't use member names as variables. Member names exist only so that you can work with an individual part of a structure.

 Don't forget to add a semicolon at the end of all structure definitions.

In Review

This chapter's goal was to teach you about structures. A *structure* is an aggregate variable data type. Whereas an array must hold values that are all the same data type, a structure can hold several values of different data types.

Before using a structure variable, you must tell C exactly what the structure looks like with a struct statement. The struct statement lets C know how many members are in the structure and the data types of each member. A structure variable is like a group of more than one variable of different data types.

Code Example

```
struct telStr {
   char lastName[15];
   char initial;
   char firstname[15];
   int areaCode;
   long int phoneNum;
   char address[25];
   char city[10];
   char state[3];   /* Leaves 1 for the null zero! */
   char zip[6];
};
main()
{
   int i;
   struct telStr friends[50];
```

Code Analysis

This code might be the start of a program that tracks telephone numbers and addresses of your friends. The code first describes a structure that has nine members. The members are made up of character arrays, a character member, an integer member, and a long integer member.

The program that begins in `main()` defines an array of 50 structure variables. (An `int` variable is also defined just to show you that structures are defined in the same location as other variables.) Each of the 50 structure variables has the `telStr` layout.

Can My Programs Save Stuff on Disk?

With Sequential Files

None of the programs you've seen so far have been able to store data for very long. Think about this for a moment: If you defined an integer variable and put a 14 in it, then turned off the computer (believe me now and try it later), that variable would no longer have 14 in it! If you turned your computer back on and tried to find the variable—no way.

This chapter explains how to save data to your disk. Once the data is on your disk, it will be there until you change or erase it. Data on your disk is just like music on a tape. You can turn off the tape deck and the tape will hold the music until you change it.

HMM... Files are critical to computer data programs. How useful would a word processor be without files?

Disk Files

Fun Fact
Before the days of floppy disks, computers stored data on punch cards.

Disks hold data in *files*. You already understand the concept of files if you've stored a C program on a disk. Files can hold either programs or data. Your programs must be loaded from the disk into memory before you can run them. You also must load data from the disk file into variables before you can work with the data. The variables also hold data before the data goes to a disk file.

There are two types of files—*sequential-access* and *random-access*. Their types determine how you can access them. If you work with a sequential-access file, you have to read or write the file in the order of the data. In a random-access file, you can jump around, reading and writing anyplace throughout the file.

PSST! A sequential file is like a cassette tape and a random-access file is like a record or a CD. You have to play songs in sequence on a tape (or fast-forward through them in order), whereas you can skip around in the music on a record or a CD.

All disk files have names that conform to the same naming rules as program names. Before you can use a disk file, whether it be to create, read, or change the data in the file, you must *open* the file.

PSST! As with a filing cabinet, you can't use a disk file without opening the file. Instead of pulling out a drawer, your computer attaches something called a *file pointer* to the file and makes sure that the disk is properly set up to hold the file you specify.

Opening a File

To open a file, you must use the `fopen()` function, whose description is included along with `printf()`'s in `stdio.h`. Before seeing `fopen()`, you have to understand the concept of a file pointer.

YIKES!

The concept of a file pointer is easy to understand. A regular pointer simply holds the address of data in a variable. A file pointer simply holds the address (the location) of the disk file you're working with.

There is a special statement you must specify to define a file pointer. As with any variable, you can name file pointers anything you want. Suppose you want to open an employee file. Before the `fopen()`, you must define a file pointer variable. If you called the file pointer `fptr`, here is how you would define a file pointer:

```
FILE * fptr;   /* Defines a file pointer named fptr */
```

Skip This, It's Technical

Most C programmers define their file pointers before `main()`. This makes the file pointer *global*, which is a fancy term meaning that the entire program can use the file. (Most other kinds of variables are *local*, not global.) Because part of the file pointer statement is in uppercase, `FILE` is defined someplace with `#define`. `FILE` is defined in `stdio.h`, which is the primary reason you should include the `stdio.h` header file when your program uses the disk for data.

Once you define a file pointer, you can connect that pointer to a file with `fopen()`. Once you specify `fopen()`, you can then use the file throughout the rest of the program. Here is the way to open a file named `C:\EMPS.DAT`. (If you don't have a C: drive, change the `C:` in these examples to a different drive letter.)

```
#include <stdio.h>
FILE *fptr;
main()
{
   fptr = fopen("C:\\EMPS.DAT", "w");
   /* Rest of program follows */
   fclose(fptr);  /* Always close the file */
```

HMM... Close your filing cabinet drawers when you're done with your files or you'll hit your head! Close all open files after you're through with them or you could lose some data. `fclose()` is the opposite of `fopen()`. In its parentheses it requires a file pointer of the file you want to close.

PSST! Once you open a file, you never have to refer to the file by name again—only by the file pointer.

 **YIKES!**

If the file pointer equals 0, you'll know that an error happened (such as a disk drive door being open).

The `"w"` (the second argument in `fopen()`) means *write*. The second argument of `fopen()` must be one of the string *mode* values found in Table 26.1.

Table 26.1. **The basic `fopen()` mode strings.**

Mode	Description
`"w"`	*Write* mode that creates a new file whether it exists or not
`"r"`	*Read* mode that lets you read an existing file. If the file doesn't exist, you get an error.
`"a"`	*Append* mode that lets you add to the end of a file or create the file if it doesn't already exist

Using Sequential Files

There are only three things you ever do with a sequential file: create it, read it, and add to it (write to it). To write to a file, you can use `fprintf()`. `fprintf()` is easy because it's just a `printf()` with a file pointer. The following code creates a file and writes some data to it using `fprintf()`:

```
#include <stdio.h>
FILE * fptr;
main()
{
   int age = 45;   /* Simple variables to write */
   float salary = 29670.50;
   fptr = fopen("C:\\MYDATA.DAT", "w"); /* Opens for output */
   fprintf(fptr, "Here is some stuff:\n");
   fprintf(fptr, "I am %d years old.\n", age);
   fprintf(fptr, "I make $%.2f dollars every three months!",
           salary);
   fclose(fptr);   /* ALWAYS close your files */
   return 0;
}
```

The contents of the file can be read with `fgets()`. `fgets()` is nothing more than a `gets()` that you can direct to a disk file. `fgets()` requires that you specify a maximum string length for the array you're reading into. You might read past the end of the file (producing an error) if you're not careful. The following code shows you how to read a file that contains string data and check for end-of-file (with the `feof()` function) along the way:

```
#include <stdio.h>
FILE * fptr;
main()
{
   char fileLine[81];   /* Will hold the output */
   fptr = fopen("C:\\MYDATA.DAT", "r");   /* Opens for input */
   if (fptr != 0)
   {   while (!feof(fptr))   /* Probably the only good
                                      use for ! */
         { fgets(fileLine, 81, fptr);   /* Gets no more
                                            than 81 chars */
            if (!feof(fptr))
               { puts(fileLine); }
```

```
        }
    } else {printf("\nError opening file.\n"); }

    fclose(fptr);   /* ALWAYS close your files */
    return 0;
}
```

YIKES!

In the `fprintf()` function, the file pointer goes at the beginning of the function. In the `fgets()` function, the file pointer goes at the *end*. There's nothing like consistency!

PSST! There is also an `fscanf()` you can use to read individual numeric values from a data file if you wrote the values with a corresponding `fprintf()`.

You can add to a file by opening the file in append mode and outputting data to it. The following program adds the line `That's all!` to the end of the `MYDATA.DAT` data file:

```
#include <stdio.h>
FILE * fptr;
main()
{
    fptr = fopen("C:\\MYDATA.DAT", "a"); /* Opens for append */
    fprintf(fptr, "\nThat's all!\n");  /* Adds the line */
    fclose(fptr);  /* ALWAYS close your files */
    return 0;
}
```

PSST! To write to a printer instead of the screen, open the DOS printer device named LPT1: or LPT2: and use that device name as the first argument of `fprint()`.

Happy Landings

 Store long-term data in data files.

Open a file with `fopen()` before you use it.

 Always close a file with `fclose()` when you're done.

Shot Down

Don't read from a file without checking for `feof()` because you might have previously read the last line in the file.

Don't forget that the file pointer goes at the *beginning* of `fprintf()` and that `fputs()` requires a file pointer at the *end* of its argument list.

In Review

The goal of this chapter was to show you how to create, read, and write sequential files. Your C program must open a file before data can be written to or read from the file. When your program is done with a file, the program should close the file.

When reading from a file, you must check for the end-of-file condition to ensure that you don't try to read past the end of the file. The `feof()` function is a built-in C function that you use to check for the end of the file.

Code Example

```
#include <stdio.h>
FILE * tvFile;
main()
{
   char name[] = "Chris";
   char show[] = "Sign Field";
   char age = 18;
```

```
tvFile = fopen("C:\\SHOWS.DAT", "w");  /* Opens for
                                           output */
if (tvFile != 0)
  { fprintf(tvFile, "My name is %s.\n", name);
    fprintf(tvFile, "My favorite TV show is %s.\n", show);
    fprintf(tvFile, "I am %d years old.", age);
    fclose(tvFile);
  }
else
  { printf("There's a problem with opening the file.\n"); }
return 0;
}
```

Code Analysis

This code describes a complete program that stores several messages in a sequential file. First the file pointer is defined, and then some data is stored in variables.

The file is then opened. If there was not an error during the open process, three messages are written to the disk before the file is closed.

This program is simple, yet it forms the beginning of a more complete database program you might want to write. Instead of assigning data to the variables directly, you might want to ask the user for the values and store the data entered by the user.

Is There Another Way to Save Files?

Use Random Files

This chapter shows you how to skip around in a file, reading and writing data as you go. The preceding chapter introduced methods you can use to write, read, or append data to a file. The problem is that once you open a sequential file for reading, you can *only* read it. There might be times when you want to read a customer structure from disk and change the customer's balance. You certainly wouldn't want to have to create a new file just so that you could write that one change. Instead, you'd want to read the customer information into a variable, change it, then write it back to disk exactly where it first resided.

The type of file you work with, either random or sequential, doesn't depend on the physical layout of the file. You can create a file sequentially and then read and change it randomly. To C, a file is just a stream of bytes, and the way you access it isn't linked to any format of the file.

Opening Random Files

To read or write a file randomly, you must open the file randomly. Table 27.1 lists the modes that access random files. As you can see, the cornerstone of random-access files is the use of the plus sign, +.

HMM...   As with sequential files, the access mode is a string that appears as the last argument of `fopen()`. Close open random files with `fclose()`, just as you do with sequential files.

Table 27.1. The random-access `fopen()` modes.

Mode	Description
`"r+"`	Opens an existing file for both reading and writing.
`"w+"`	Opens a new file for writing and reading.
`"a+"`	Opens a file in append mode (the file pointer points to the end of the file) but lets you move back through the file, reading and writing as you go.

Moving Around in a File

Use the `fseek()` function to move around in a file. After you open a file, C initializes the file pointer to point to the next place in the file you can read or write. `fseek()` moves the file pointer so that you can read and write at places that would normally not be pointed at. Here is the format of `fseek()`:

```
fseek(filePtr, longVal, origin);
```

The *filePtr* is the file pointer used in the `fopen()` function that used a random-access mode. The *longVal* is a `long int` variable or literal that can be either positive or negative. The *longVal* is the number of bytes to skip forward or backward in the file. The *origin* is always one of the values in Table 27.2. *origin* tells `fseek()` where to start seeking from.

Table 27.2. `origin` values that can appear in `fseek()`.

origin	Description
SEEK_SET	Beginning of file
SEEK_CUR	Current file location
SEEK_END	End of file

PSST! Use `fseek()` for random-access files only. Sequential files can be accessed only in the order of their data.

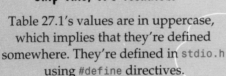

Skip This, It's Technical

Table 27.1's values are in uppercase, which implies that they're defined somewhere. They're defined in `stdio.h` using `#define` directives.

The following program opens a file for random-access mode, writes the letters A through Z to it, then rereads those letters backwards. The file doesn't have to be reopened before the reading begins because of the random-access mode `"w+"`.

```c
#include <stdio.h>
FILE * fptr;
main()
{
   char letter;
   int i;
   fptr = fopen("C:\\LETTERS.DAT", "w+");  /* Opens for
                                              write, then
                                              read */
   for (letter = 'A'; letter <= 'Z'; letter++)
   { fputc(letter, fptr);
   }
   /* Now reads the file backwards */
   fseek(fptr, -1, SEEK_END);  /* Minus 1 byte from the end */
   printf("Here is the file backwards:\n");
   for (i = 26; i > 0; i--)
   { letter = fgetc(fptr);
      fseek(fptr, -2, SEEK_CUR);  /* Reads a letter, then
                                     backs up 2 */
     printf("The next letter is %c\n", letter);
   }
   fclose(fptr);
   return 0;
}
```

PSST! As you can see, `fputc()` is a great function for outputting individual characters to a file. `fgetc()` reads individual characters from a file.

YIKES!

You might not see a use yet for random-access files. Random access offers you the advantage of writing data to a file, then rereading the same data without closing and opening the file. Also, `fseek()` lets you position the file pointer any number of bytes from the beginning, middle, or end of the file.

Assuming that the file of letters still resides on the disk from the last program, this next program asks the user which position he or she wants to change. The program then positions the file pointer with `fseek()` and writes an * at that point before `fseek()`ing to the beginning of the file and printing it again.

```c
#include <stdio.h>
FILE * fptr;
main()
{
    char letter;
    int i;
    fptr = fopen("C:\\LETTERS.DAT", "r+");  /* Opens for read,
                                               then write */
    printf("What is the position you want to change? ");
    scanf(" %d", &i);
    /* Seeks to that location from the beginning of the file */
    fseek(fptr, (i - 1), SEEK_SET);  /* Subtracts 1 because
                                        first position is 0 */
    /* Writes '*' over that position */
    fputc('*', fptr);
    /* Now prints the file */
    fseek(fptr, 0, SEEK_SET);  /* Back to the beginning */
    printf("Here is the file now:\n");
    for (i = 0; i < 26; i++)
```

```
  { letter = fgetc(fptr);
    printf("The next letter is %c\n", letter);
  }
  fclose(fptr);
  return 0;
}
```

The program prints the contents of the file after the * is written at
the position indicated by the user.

Happy Landings

 Use a plus sign, +, in the fopen() mode string if you need to
change data in a file.

 Remember that fseek() moves a file pointer all around a
random file so that you can read or write from the beginning,
middle, or end.

Shot Down

 Don't forget to close a file when you are done with it.

In Review

The goal of this chapter was to explain how random-access files
work. Once you open a file in random-access mode, you can read
and write to that file in any order you need to. The fseek() function
is the built-in function that skips around the file from position to
position.

Being able to change the contents of a file is important when you
want to update file data. Often you will want to change a person's
address, change an inventory item's quantity, and so on without
rewriting the entire file as you'd have to if you used sequential file
processing.

Code Example

```c
#include <stdio.h>
struct std {
   char id[4];  /* 3-character ID plus a null zero */
   float avg;
};
FILE *gradePtr;
main()
{
   struct std students;  /* Student records */
   gradePtr = fopen("C:\\GRADES.DAT", "w+");
   do {
     printf("What is the next student's 3-character ID?\n");
     printf("Enter Q to quit entering students): ");
     gets(students.id);
     if (students.id[0] != 'Q')
       { printf("What is the student's average? ");
         scanf(" %f", &students);
         getchar();  /* Gets rid of the Enter keypress */
         fprintf(gradePtr, "%s%.1f\n", students.id,
                 students.avg); }
   } while (students.id[0] != 'Q');
   fclose(gradePtr);
   return 0;
}
```

Code Analysis

This code contains a complete program that writes structure data
to a random-access file. The program could have just as easily
written to a sequential file, but the `fprintf()` ensures that each
structure written to the disk has the same format and length—
a three-character string followed by a floating-point value.

You can easily write the code to read or change any record in the file
using this `fseek()`:

```c
fseek(gradePtr, recNo * sizeof(struct std), SEEK_SET);
```

in which `recNo` is a record number that the user wants to change.

Part 5
Form Follows Function

Mayday! Mayday! She's going down!

How Can I Better Organize My Programs?

Using Functions

Typical computer programs are not the 20-to-30-line variety that you see in textbooks. In the "real world," computer programs are much longer. If you were to put an entire program in main(), it would take a lot of effort to find anything specific if you later needed to change the program. This chapter is the first of three chapters that explore ways to partition your programs into sections via multiple functions. Categorizing your code by breaking it into sections makes programs easier to write and also easier to maintain.

YIKES!

People have to write, change, and fix code. The clearer you make the code by writing lots of functions that do individual tasks, the faster you can get home from your programming job and relax!

Form Follows C Functions

As you might know, C programs aren't like BASIC programs. C was designed to force you to think in a modular style through the use of functions. A BASIC program is often just one very long program that isn't broken into separate routines. (Some of the newer versions of BASIC, such as QBasic, offer almost the same functionality that C offers.) A C program isn't just one long program. It's made up of many routines called functions. One of them (the one usually listed first) is named main().

If your program does very much, break it into several functions. Each function should do one primary task. For instance, if you were writing a C program to get a list of numbers from the keyboard, then sort them, then print them to the screen, you *could* write all of this in one big function, all in main(), as the following program outline shows:

```
main()
{
    /* This is not a working program, just an outline */
      :
    /* C code to retrieve a list of numbers */
      :
    /* C code to sort the numbers */
      :
    /* C code to print the sorted list on-screen */
      :
    return 0;
}
```

This program does *not* offer a good format for the tasks you want accomplished. Even though this program wouldn't take many lines of code, it's much better to get in the habit of breaking every program into distinct tasks. You shouldn't use main() to do everything. In fact, you should use main() to do very little except call each of the other functions. A better way to organize this program would be to write separate functions for each task that the program is to do.

Fun Fact
Breaking programs into smaller functions is called structured programming.

 **HMM...** Of course, every function shouldn't be a single line, but make sure that each function acts as a building block and performs only a single task.

Here is a better outline for the program just described:

```
main()
{  getNums();     /* Calls a function that gets the numbers */
   sortNums();    /* Sorts the numbers */
   printNums();   /* Prints the numbers on-screen */
   return 0;      /* Quits the program */
}
getNums()
{   :
   /* C code to retrieve a list of numbers */
   return;
}
sortNums()
```

```
{   :
   /* C code to sort the numbers */
   return;
}
printNums()
{   :
   /* C code to print the sorted list on-screen */
   return;
}
```

Even though this program outline is longer than the previous one, this one's better. The only thing that `main()` does is control the other functions by showing an overview of how they're called.

Each separate function does its thing, then returns to `main()`, where `main()` calls the next function until there are no more functions. `main()` then returns to DOS.

A good rule of thumb is that a function should not take more lines than will fit on a single screen. If the function is longer than that, you're probably making it do too much.

Any function can call any other function. For example, if you wanted `printNums()` to print a title with your name and the date at the top of the page, you might have `printNums()` call another function named `printTitle()`. `printTitle()` would then return to `printNums()` when it was finished.

Look at all the functions in the Blackjack game in Appendix B. The program is only a few pages long but it contains several functions. Look through the code and see if you can find a function that calls another function located elsewhere in the program.

Local or Global?

The program outline explained in the preceding section needs more code to work. Before being able to add code, you need to take a closer look at variable definitions. In C, all variables can be either *local* or *global.* All the variables you have seen so far have been local. Most of the time, a local variable is safer than a global variable because a local variable offers itself on a *need-to-know access.* That is, if a function needs a variable, it can have access to another function's local variables. If a function doesn't need to access another function's local variable, it can't have access. Any function can read, change, and zero-out global variables, so they don't offer as much safety.

The following rules describe the difference between local and global variables:

 A variable is global if and only if you define the variable (such as `int i;`) before a function name.

 A variable is local if and only if you define it after an opening brace. A function always begins with opening braces. Some statements, such as `while`, also have opening braces, and you can define local variables within those braces as well.

PSST! An opening and closing brace enclose what is known as a *block.*

Given these rules, it should be obvious that `l1` and `l2` are local variables and that `g1` and `g2` are global variables in the following program:

```
#include <stdio.h>
int g1 = 10;
main()
{
    float l1;
    l1 = 9.0;
```

```
        printf("%d %f\n", g1, l1); /* Prints global g1 and local */
        prAgain();                 /* l1, calls next function,  */
        return 0;                  /* and returns to DOS        */
    }
    float g2 = 9.0;  /* A global variable */
    prAgain()
    {
        int l2 = 5;
        printf("%d %f %d\n", l2, g2, g1);  /* Can't print l1! */
        return;
    }
```

YIKES!

You probably don't yet understand the `return 0` statement. To make matters worse, `return` by itself is used at the end of the `prAgain()` function. The reasoning is explained in the next two chapters.

PSST! The variable g2 is global because it's defined before a function (`prAgain()`).

Local variables are usable *only* within their own block of code. Therefore, l1 could never be printed or changed in `prAgain()`, because l1 is local to `main()`. Conversely, l2 could never be used in `main()` because l2 is visible only to `prAgain()`. The variable g1 is visible to the entire program. g2 is visible only from its point of definition *down.*

PSST! All global variables are known from their points of definition *down* in the source file. Don't define a global variable in the middle of a program (as is done in the preceding program) because its definition can be too hard to find during debugging sessions. You should limit (or eliminate) the use of globals. If you use them at all, define all of them before `main()`.

HMM... There is a problem with the program outline shown earlier. If you use only local variables (and you should always try to), the variable values input in `getNums()` can be neither sorted in `sortNums()` nor printed in `printNums()`! Stay tuned, because the next chapter shows you the solution.

YIKES!

If you receive a compiler warning about a call to a function without a prototype, ignore it for now. Your questions will be answered in Chapter 30.

Happy Landings

- Define local variables after a block's opening brace. Define global variables before a function begins.

- Local variables are safer than global variables, so use local variables as much as possible.

- Break your programs into lots of functions to ease maintenance and speed development time.

Shot Down

 Don't define global variables in the middle of a program. They're too hard to locate if you do.

In Review

The goal of this chapter was to teach you the building-block approach to writing C programs. Long programs can become unwieldy unless you break them into several separate functions. One long `main()` function is analogous to a long book without chapter divisions. Break your long programs into separate functions, and have each function perform a single, separate task in the program.

Once you divide your programs into several functions, you have to consider how variables are used throughout the code. Local variables are defined inside a function and are usable only in that function. The opposite of a local variable is a global variable, whose value is usable in all functions after its definition. Global variables are frowned upon. Local variables are safer because you can limit their access to only those functions that need to use them. In the next chapter, you'll learn how to share local variables between functions.

Code Example

```
#include <stdio.h>
char name[] = "Mary";
main()
{
   int age = 25;  /* Local variable */
   /* The following printf() can use name
      because name is global */
   printf("%s is %d years old.\n", name, age);
   nextFun();  /* Calls second function */
   return 0;   /* and returns to DOS    */
}
float weight = 119.0;  /* A global variable */
nextFun()
```

```
{
    /* The next printf() CANNOT print age because
       age is local and usable only in main() */
    printf("%s is %d years old and weighs %.0f pounds.\n",
           name, age, weight);
    return;   /* Goes back and finishes main() */
}
```

Code Analysis

This program contains three variables, two of which are global (`name` and `weight`) and one that is local to `main()` (`age`). The first function, `main()`, is put on hold when it calls `nextFun()`. When `nextFun()` concludes, the last line in `main()` is free to finish.

The `nextFun()` function can't use the value of `age` because `age` is local to `main()` and therefore usable only in `main()`.

How Do
Functions
Share Data?

By Passing Variables

The preceding chapter left some questions unanswered. If multiple functions are good (they are), and if local variables are good (they are), then you must have a way to share local variables between functions that need to share them. You don't want *all* functions to have access to *all* variables, because not every function needs access to every variable. If full variable access between functions were needed, you might as well use global variables.

To share data from function to function, you must *pass* variables from function to function. When one function passes a variable to another function, only those two functions have access to the variable (assuming the variable is local). This chapter explains how to pass variables between functions.

Passing Arguments

When you pass a variable from one function to another, you are *passing an argument* from the first function to the next. You can pass more than one variable at a time. The receiving function *receives the parameters* from the function that sent the variables.

YIKES!

The words *variable, argument,* and *parameter* are sometimes used interchangeably when passing and receiving values. The name is not as important as understanding what is happening. Figure 29.1 helps explain these terms.

Figure 29.1.

Getting the terms correct.

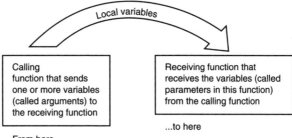

Local variables

Calling
function that sends
one or more variables
(called arguments) to
the receiving function

Receiving function that
receives the variables (called
parameters in this function)
from the calling function

...to here

From here...

Methods of Passing Arguments

There are two ways to pass arguments from a function to another
function. You can pass arguments *by value* and *by address*. Both of
these methods pass arguments *to* a receiving function from a calling
function. There is also a way to *return* a value from a function back
to the calling function that you'll read about in the next chapter.

PSST!

All this passing of values talk focuses on the parentheses
that follow function names. That's right, those empty
parentheses have a use after all! The variables you want to
pass go inside the parentheses of the function call, and also
in the receiving function, as you'll see in the next section.

HMM...

Yes, this passing values stuff is important! It's easy,
though, as you'll see.

Passing by Value

Sometimes *passing by value* is called *passing by copy*. You'll hear them used interchangeably because they mean the same thing. Passing by value means that the *value* of the variable is passed to the receiving function, not the variable itself. Here is a program that passes a value from `main()` to `half()`:

```c
#include <stdio.h>
main()
{   int i;
    printf("Please enter a number... ");
    scanf(" %d", &i);
    /* Now, passes the variable to a function */
    half(i);  /* i is passed by value */
    printf("In main(), i is still %d.\n", i);
    return 0;  /* Goes back to DOS */
}
half(int i)  /* Receives value of i */
{
    i = i / 2;  /* Halves i */
    printf("Your value halved is %d.\n", i);
    return;  /* Returns to main() */
}
```

Here is the program's output:

```
Please enter a number... 12
Your value halved is 6.
In main(), i is still 12.
```

Notice that you must put the data type inside the receiving function's parameter list. If you passed more than one variable separated by commas, all would have to have their data types listed as well, even if they were all the same type. As Figure 29.2 shows, the contents of i are passed to `half()`. The i in `main()` is never changed *because only a copy of its value is passed.*

Figure 29.2.

The value of i is passed, not the variable i.

```
main( )
{
    int i;
    /* Prompt and input code go here*/
    half(i);     value of i
    return 0;
}
                        half(int i)
                        {
                            i = i / 2
                            printf( /*Rest of printf()*/
                            return;
                        }
```

Skip This, It's Technical

Passing by value protects a variable. If the receiving function changes a passed-by-value variable, the calling function's variable is left unchanged. Therefore, passing by value is always safe because the receiving function can't change the passing function's variables—only use them.

HMM... If the receiving function called its parameter i, the program would still work the way it does now. The i would be local to half(), whereas the i in main() would be local to main(). *The i's would be local to two different functions and therefore would be distinct.*

C uses the passing by value method for all non-array variables. Therefore, if you pass any variable that is not an array to a function, only a copy of that variable's value is passed. The variable will be left unchanged in the calling function no matter what the called function does with the value.

Passing by Address

When you pass an array to another function, the array is passed by address. Instead of a copy of the array being passed, the memory address of the array is passed. The receiving function then places its receiving parameter array *over* the address passed. The bottom line is that the receiving function works with the same address as the calling function. If the receiving function changes one of the variables in the parameter list, *the calling function's argument changes as well.*

The following program passes an array to a function. The function puts x throughout the array and then `main()` prints the array. Notice that `main()` prints all xs because the function changed the argument.

```
#include <stdio.h>
#include <string.h>
main()
{  char name[15] = "Chris Williams";
   change(name);
   printf("Back in main(), the name is now %s.\n", name);
   return 0;
}
change(char name[15])
{
   strcpy(name, "xxxxxxxxxxxxxx");
   return;
}
```

This program produces the following output:

```
Back in main(), the name is now xxxxxxxxxxxxxx.
```

If you want to override the passing of non-arrays by value, you can force C to pass regular non-array variables by address. However, doing so looks really crazy! Here is a program, similar to the first one you saw in this chapter, that produces a different output:

```
#include <stdio.h>
main()
{  int i;
   printf("Please enter a number... ");
   scanf(" %d", &i);
   /* Now, passes the variable to a function */
```

```
   half(&i);  /* i is passed by address */
   printf("In main(), i is now %d.\n", i);
   return 0;  /* Goes back to DOS */
}
half(int *i)  /* Receives address of i */
{
   *i = *i / 2;  /* Halves i */
   printf("Your value halved is %d.\n", *i);
   return;  /* Returns to main() */
}
```

Here is the output from the program:

```
Please enter a number... 12
Your value halved is 6.
In main(), i is now 6.
```

YIKES!

It looks strange, but if you want to pass a non-array by address, precede it in the passing function with an & (address-of) symbol and then put a * (dereferencing) symbol in front of the variable *everywhere it appears* in the receiving function. If you think you're now passing a pointer to a function, you're exactly right.

PSST! Now scanf() is not so unfamiliar. Remember that you put an & before non-array variables but not before array variables that you pass to scanf(). When you call scanf(), you must pass it the address of variables so that scanf() can change the variables. Because strings are arrays, when you get a string from the keyboard, you don't put an address-of operator before the array name.

The next chapter finishes up passing of values between functions by showing you how to return a value from one function to another. Also, you will finally understand the true use of stdio.h.

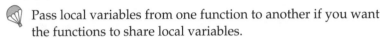

Happy Landings

 Pass local variables from one function to another if you want the functions to share local variables.

Pass variables by value if you want their values protected from the called function.

Pass variables by address if you want their values changed by the called function.

Place an & before non-array variables you want to pass by address. Leave off the & if you want to pass arrays.

Shot Down

Don't try to pass a non-array variable by value. There is no way to do that in C.

In Review

The goal of this chapter was to show you how to share local variables between functions. When one function needs access to a local variable defined in another function, you must pass that variable. The parentheses after function names contain the variables you're passing and receiving.

Normally you pass non-array variables *by value,* which means that the receiving function can use them but not affect their values in the calling function. Arrays are passed *by address,* which means that if the receiving function changes them, the array variables are also changed in the calling function. You can pass non-array variables by address by preceding them with the address-of operator, &, and receiving them with the dereference operator, *.

Code Example

```c
#include <stdio.h>
main()
{
   int i, j, k;
   printf("I'll add three variables. \n");
   printf("Please enter the first number: ");
   scanf(" %d", &i);
   printf("Please enter the second number: ");
   scanf(" %d", &j);
   printf("Please enter the third number: ");
   scanf(" %d", &k);
   addThem(i, j, k);  /* Passes variables by value */
   return 0;  /* Goes back to DOS */
}
addThem(int i, int j, int k)
{
   int total;  /* Local to this function */
   total = i + j + k;
   printf("\nThe total of the three variables is %d.\n",
          total);
   return 0;  /* Returns to main() */
}
```

Code Analysis

This program accepts three variables in `main()` and then prints their total in the `addThem()` function. The variables are passed by value to `addThem()`. When a function receives variables, as done here, you must put the data type in front of each of them. The following is *not* allowed for the first line of `addThem()`:

```c
addThem(int i, j, k)   /* Invalid. int is required
                          three times */
```

The local variable `total` holds the sum of the three passed variables. After the total is printed, control is returned to `main()`. The `0` that you see following the `return` statements in this book's programs will finally be explained in the next chapter.

How Can
I Perfect
My Functions?

Using Return Values and Prototypes

This chapter is not the end of your C learning. This chapter marks only the beginning. Sounds deep, doesn't it? This chapter completes the multiple-function picture by showing you how to return values from the called function to the calling function. Finally, function *prototypes* are explained.

The bottom line is this: You will now understand why most programs in this book contain this line:

```
return 0;
```

and you will understand the true purpose of header files.

Returning Values

So far you've seen how to send variables *to* functions. You're now ready to learn how to return a value. When a function is to return a value, use the `return` statement to return the value. Often, C programmers put parentheses after the `return` statement, with the return value inside those parentheses, such as `return (answer);`.

 **HMM...** If a function doesn't return a value, a `return` statement isn't needed because the function will return to the calling function automatically. Nevertheless, if you need to return a value, a `return` statement is required.

PSST! You can return *only one value* to the calling function! There are no exceptions to this rule.

Although a single return value might seem limiting, it really is not. Consider the built-in `sqrt()` function. You might remember from

Chapter 20 that `sqrt()` returns the square root of whatever value is passed to it. `sqrt()` doesn't return several values, only one. As a matter of fact, none of the built-in functions returns more than a single value, and neither can yours.

Skip This, It's Technical

The `gets()` function seems as if it returns more than one value because it returns a character string array. Remember, though, that an array name is nothing more than a pointer to the array's first position. Therefore, `gets()` actually returns a character pointer that points to the beginning of the string entered by the user.

The following program contains a function that receives three integer values—`a`, `b`, and `c`. The function named `fMul3()` multiplies those three values by each other and then returns the answer.

```
#include <stdio.h>
long int fMul3(int var1, int var2, int var3);
main()
{
   int a, b, c;
   long int answer;
   printf("What is the first number to multiply? ");
   scanf(" %d", &a);
   printf("What is the second number to multiply? ");
   scanf(" %d", &b);
   printf("What is the third number to multiply? ");
   scanf(" %d", &c);

   answer = fMul3(a, b, c);   /* Passes three variables and
                                 returns the answer */
   printf("\nThose three values multiplied by each other "
          "equal %ld.", answer);
   /* It's okay to continue a string literal over two lines */
   return 0;
}
long int fMul3(int var1, int var2, int var3)
```

```
{
   int locAnswer;
   locAnswer = var1 * var2 * var3;
   return (locAnswer);
}
```

PSST! 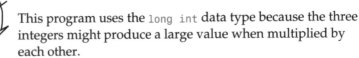 This program uses the `long int` data type because the three integers might produce a large value when multiplied by each other.

Here is a sample output from this program:

```
What is the first number to multiply? 3
What is the second number to multiply? 4
What is the third number to multiply? 5

Those three values multiplied by each other equal 60.
```

 **HMM...** Notice that `main()` assigned the `fMul3()` return value to `answer`. `main()` had to do something with the value that was returned from `fMul3()`.

The Return Data Type

At the beginning of the `fMul3()` function you see `long int`. `long int` is the data type of the returned value `locAnswer`. You *must* put the return data type before any function name that returns a value. If the function returned a `float`, `float` would have to precede the function name.

If you don't specify a return data type, C assumes `int`. Therefore, C expects that every function without a return data type specified explicitly will return `int`. *Both* of these functions' first lines mean exactly the same thing to C:

```
int myFun(int a, float x, char c)
```

and

```
myFun(int a, float x, char c)  /* int is assumed */
```

PSST! Guess what? Even `main()` is assumed to return an `int` value unless you specify an overriding return data type. *That* is why you've seen `return 0;` at the end of most of these programs! Because `main()` has no specified return data type, `int` is assumed, and the `return 0;` ensures that an `int` is returned to DOS. DOS, by the way, just ignores the return data type unless you want to use the advanced DOS `errorlevel` command to receive the 0.

If your function doesn't return a value, or if your function isn't passed a value, you can insert the keyword `void` for either the return data type or the parameter list or both. Therefore, the first line of a function that neither gets any value nor returns any value might look like this:

```
void doSomething(void)  /* Neither is passed nor returns */
```

YIKES!

`main()` can't be of type `void` in ANSI C. It must be of type `int`.

One Last Step: Prototype

There is one last step to making a function work properly. If a function returns any value other than int, you should *prototype* that function. Actually, you should prototype functions that return integers as well, except main(), which doesn't need a prototype.

The word *prototype* means a model of something else. A prototype of a function is just a model of the actual function. At first, a C prototype seems like a total waste of time.

HMM... Prototypes aren't required if you don't return a value or if you return an integer value, but they are *strongly recommended*. Once you prototype, C ensures that you don't pass a float value to a function that expects to receive a char. Without the prototype, C would try to convert the float to a char, and a bad value would be passed as a result.

To prototype a function, place an exact duplicate of the function's first line somewhere before main(). The prototype for fMul3() appears right before main() in the program you saw earlier. The line is *not* a function call because it appears before main(). The line is not a function's actual first line because of the semicolon that follows all prototypes. The line is a function prototype. If your program calls 20 functions, you should have 20 prototypes.

Prototype *every* function in your program! That means every function called by your code and *even the built-in functions like* printf(). "Huh?" might be a good question at this point. You might wonder how you can prototype printf() when you didn't write it to begin with. The file stdio.h contains a prototype for printf(), scanf(), getchar(), and many other input and output functions! The prototype for strcpy() appears in string.h. You should find out the name of the header file when you learn a new built-in function so that you can #include it and make sure that each function is prototyped.

Wrapping Things Up

Never pass or return a global variable if you use one. Global variables don't have to be passed. Also, the parameter lists in the calling function, receiving function, and prototype should match in both number and data type. (The names of the values don't have to match.)

You now know everything there is to know about passing parameters and returning values. Put on your official programmer's thinking cap and start your C compiler!

Happy Landings

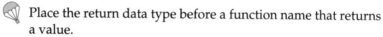 Place the return data type before a function name that returns a value.

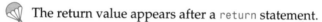 The return value appears after a `return` statement.

In the calling function, do something with the return value. Print it or assign it to something. Calling a function that returns a value is useless if you do nothing with the return value.

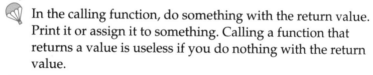 Use `void` as the return data type or in the parameter list if you neither return nor pass values to a function.

Shot Down

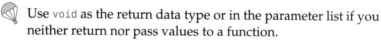 Don't try to return more than one value from a function.

Don't try to return a noninteger without a prototype. Better yet, prototype *all* functions except `main()`.

In Review

The goal of this chapter was to round out your knowledge of functions by explaining prototypes and return values. When your program contains lots of functions, prototype those functions somewhere before main(). The prototypes tell C what to expect. After you prototype, you can pass and return variables of any data type. (You can return ints only if you don't prototype.)

The prototype ensures that you don't inadvertently pass the wrong data types to functions. For example, if the prototype states that you'll pass two floats to a function, but you accidentally pass two ints, C will complain. C won't complain if you don't prototype, and you might get wrong results because of it.

Now that you know how to return values, you can write functions that mirror those that are built-in, such as sqrt() and rand(). When you call a function, that function returns a value based on the function's code. A function can return a maximum of one value, just like functions that are built-in.

Code Example

```c
#include <stdio.h>
float divideIt(float numFromMain);   /* Prototype */
main()
{
   float myNum, half;
   printf("Please type a number: ");
   scanf(" %f", &myNum);
   half = divideIt(myNum);
   printf("Your number divided by two is %.1f.\n", half);
   return 0;
}
float divideIt(float numFromMain)
{
   float halfNum;
   halfNum = numFromMain / 2.0;   /* Divides main()'s number */
   return (halfNum);   /* Sends the halved value back */
}
```

Code Analysis

This program shows how to prototype and call a function that returns one-half the value passed to it. The prototype lets C know that the function named divideIt() receives and returns a floating-point value. Because divideIt()'s local variable can't be used in main(), its value is returned to main() and captured in main()'s variable named half.

It would be more efficient to divide the value by 2 in main(), but this example better demonstrates the concepts in this chapter.

Fun Fact
If you want to learn more about C, turn to Appendix A for a list of other, more advanced C books.

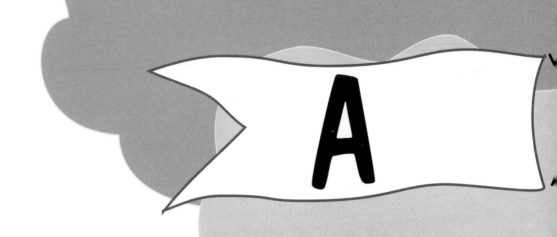

Where Do I Go from Here?

This appendix lists some books that you might want to read now that you know C. All are from Sams Publishing, and all are listed on the book order form included with this book.

Teach Yourself C in 21 Days

With this best-selling book, users can achieve C success now! Each lesson can be completed in two to three hours or less. Shaded syntax boxes, Q & A sections, and "Do/Don't" sections reinforce the important topics of C. (Beginning to Intermediate)

Advanced C

Here's the next step for programmers who want to improve their C programming skills. This book gives efficiency tips and techniques for debugging C programs and improving their speed, memory usage, and readability. (Intermediate to Advanced)

Moving from C to C++

An invaluable guide for C programmers who want to learn how to move from C to C++. This book shows how one application written in C is converted to C++ with more efficient code. It includes tips and techniques for making the transition from C to C++. It also shows the "why" of object-oriented programming before teaching the specifics. (Beginning to Intermediate)

C++ Programming 101

Readers take an active approach to learning C++ in this step-by-step tutorial/workbook. Special features such as Find the Bug, Try This, Think About..., Finish the Program, and Still Confused? give the reader a thorough understanding of the language. (Beginning)

Turbo C++ Programming 101

Readers take an active approach to learning Turbo C++ in this step-by-step tutorial/workbook. Special features such as Find the Bug, Try This, Think About..., Finish the Program, and Still Confused? give the reader a thorough understanding of the language. (Beginning)

Advanced C++

This comprehensive guide is the next step for programmers who have achieved proficiency with the basics of C++ and want to learn about advanced topics. (Intermediate to Advanced)

Playing Around with C Blackjack

Programming is not all work and no play, and the following Black-jack game proves it! The game provides a long example that you can study as you master C. Although the game has been kept extremely simple, a lot happens in this program.

As with all well-written programs, this one is commented thoroughly. You will find more and more of the program understandable as you progress through this book. One of the reasons the program is kept simple is to keep it compiler-independent. For example, there is no screen-clearing routine. The comments in the function named `dispTitle()` explain what you might want to do to add a fancier screen-clearing routine than the generic one provided. Also, you might want to find out how your C compiler produces colors on the screen so that you can add pizazz to the game's display.

PSST!   Once you master enough of C to understand the program's inner workings, you'll want to explore graphics capabilities and actually draw the cards.

Numbers appear to the left of many code lines. These are the numbers of the chapters that discuss the concepts used in the lines. If a line confuses you, refer to the appropriate chapter.

```
1   /* Filename: BLAKJACK.C

3       This program plays a game of Blackjack with you. The
        computer is the dealer and you are the victim—er, I mean
        player. The dealer gets a card that you can see. The dealer
        then asks if you want another card by asking "Hit" or
        "Stand." If you choose to hit, the dealer gives you another
        card. If you choose to stand, the dealer draws or stands,
        and the game is played out according to the cards you and
        the dealer have. As with real Blackjack, the dealer stands
        on 17. The winner is announced only after both the player's
        and the dealer's hands are finished. */

    /***************************************************************
     ANSI C standard header files appear next */
7   #include <stdio.h>
    #include <time.h>
    #include <ctype.h>
    #include <stdlib.h>

    /***************************************************************
     Defined constants appear next */
7   #define BELL '\a'
    #define DEALER 0
    #define PLAYER 1

    /* Must keep two sets of totals for dealer and for player. The
       first set counts Aces as 1 and the second counts Aces as
       11. Unlike "real world" Blackjack, this program doesn't
       allow some Aces to be 1 while others Aces are 11 in the
       same hand. */
7   #define ACELOW 0
    #define ACEHIGH 1
```

```
     /* Only one global variable is used in this entire program.
        The variable holds 0, which means false initially. Once the
        user enters his or her name in initCardsScreen(), this
        variable is set to 1 (for true), so the name is never asked
        for again the rest of the program. */
 5   int askedForName = 0;   /* False initially */
     /***************************************************************
      This program's specific prototypes */
30   void dispTitle(void);
     void initCardsScreen(int cards[52], int playerPoints[2],
                          int dealerPoints[2], int total[2],
                          int * numCards);
     int  dealCard(int * numCards, int cards[52]);
     void dispCard(int cardDrawn, int points[2]);
     void totalIt(int points[2], int total[2], int who);
     void dealerGetsCard(int *numCards, int cards[52],
                                       int dealerPoints[2]);
     void playerGetsCard(int *numCards, int cards[52],
                                       int playerPoints[2]);
     char getAns(char mesg[]);
     void findWinner(int total[2]);

     /***************************************************************
      C's program execution always begins at main() here */
 2   main()
     {
 5      int numCards;   /* Equals 52 at beginning of each game */
21      int cards[52], playerPoints[2], dealerPoints[2], total[2];
        char ans;   /* For user's Hit/Stand or Yes/No response */
14      do { initCardsScreen(cards, playerPoints, dealerPoints,
23                         total, &numCards);
29         dealerGetsCard(&numCards, cards, dealerPoints);
 4         printf("\n");   /* Prints a blank line */
29         playerGetsCard(&numCards, cards, playerPoints);
           playerGetsCard(&numCards, cards, playerPoints);
14         do {
29            ans = getAns("Hit or stand (H/S)? ");
11            if (ans == 'H')
29               { playerGetsCard(&numCards, cards,
                              playerPoints);
               }
           } while (ans != 'S');
29         totalIt(playerPoints, total, PLAYER);
                                        /* Player's total */
14         do {
29            dealerGetsCard(&numCards, cards, dealerPoints);
```

```
              } while (dealerPoints[ACEHIGH] < 17);
                                  /* 17: Dealer stops */
              totalIt(dealerPoints, total, DEALER);
                                  /* Dealer's total */
              findWinner(total);
              ans = getAns("\nPlay again (Y/N)? ");
            } while (ans == 'Y');
30     return;
     }


 3  /***********************************************************
     This function initializes the face values of the deck of
     cards by putting four sets of 1-13 in the 52-card array. Also
     clears the screen and displays a title. */
28  void initCardsScreen(int cards[52], int playerPoints[2],
                         int dealerPoints[2], int total[2],
                         int *numCards)
     {
 5     int sub, val = 1;  /* This function's Work variables */
 6     char firstName[15];  /* Holds user's first name */
23     *numCards = 52;  /* Holds running total of
                               number of cards */
15     for (sub = 0; sub <= 51; sub++)  {  /* Counts from
                                          0 to 51 */
13       val = (val == 14) ? 1 : val; /* If val is 14,
                                          reset to 1 */
21       cards[sub] = val;
13       val++;  }
15     for (sub = 0; sub <= 1; sub++) /* Counts from 0 to 1 */
 9       { playerPoints[sub]=dealerPoints[sub]=total[sub]=0; }
29     dispTitle();
11     if (askedForName == 0)  /* Name asked for only once */
 4       { printf("\nWhat is your first name? ");
 8         scanf(" %s", firstName);
 5         askedForName = 1;  /* Don't ask prompt again */
 4         printf("Ok, %s, get ready for casino action!\n\n",
                   firstName);
18         getchar();  /* Discards newline. You can safely */
       }              /* ignore compiler warning here.    */
30     return;
     }


 3  /***********************************************************
     This function gets a card for the player and updates the
     player's points. */
28  void playerGetsCard(int *numCards, int cards[52],
                                    int playerPoints[2])
     {
```

```
 5      int newCard;
29      newCard = dealCard(numCards, cards);
 4      printf("You draw: ");
29      dispCard(newCard, playerPoints);
      }

 3    /*************************************************************
      This function gets a card for the dealer and updates the
      dealer's points. */
28    void dealerGetsCard(int *numCards, int cards[52],
                                      int dealerPoints[2])
      {
 5      int newCard;
29      newCard = dealCard(numCards, cards);
 4      printf("The dealer draws: ");
29      dispCard(newCard, dealerPoints);
      }

 3    /*************************************************************
      This function gets a card from the deck and stores it in
      either the dealer's or the player's hold of cards. */
      int dealCard(int * numCards, int cards[52])
      {
 5      int cardDrawn, subDraw;
        time_t t;  /* Gets time for a random value */
20      srand(time(&t));  /* Seeds random-number generator */
        subDraw = (rand() % (*numCards));  /* From 0 to numcards */
        cardDrawn = cards[subDraw];
24      cards[subDraw] = cards[*numCards - 1];  /* Puts top card */
23      (*numCards)--;                          /* in place of drawn one */
30      return cardDrawn;
      }

 3    /*************************************************************
      Displays the last-drawn card and updates points with it. */
28    void dispCard(int cardDrawn, int points[2])
      {
17      switch (cardDrawn) {
        case(11) : printf("%s\n", "Jack");
10                 points[ACELOW] += 10;
21                 points[ACEHIGH] += 10;
16                 break;
        case(12) : printf("%s\n", "Queen");
10                 points[ACELOW] += 10;
21                 points[ACEHIGH] += 10;
16                 break;
```

```
              case(13) : printf("%s\n", "King");
10                       points[ACELOW] += 10;
21                       points[ACEHIGH] += 10;
16                       break;
            default :  points[ACELOW] += cardDrawn;
11                     if (cardDrawn == 1)
                          { printf("%s\n", "Ace");
10                          points[ACEHIGH] += 11;
                          }
                       else
10                        { points[ACEHIGH] += cardDrawn;
4                           printf("%d\n", cardDrawn); }
            }
30      return;
     }


3    /**************************************************************
        Figures the total for player or dealer to see who won. This
        function takes into account the fact that Ace is either 1
        or 11. */
28   void totalIt(int points[2], int total[2], int who)
     {
3       /* The following routine first looks to see if the total
           points counting Aces as 1 is equal to the total points
           counting Aces as 11. If so, or if the total points
           counting Aces as 11 is more than 21, the program uses
           the total with Aces as 1 only. */
11      if ((points[ACELOW] == points[ACEHIGH]) ||
            (points[ACEHIGH] > 21))
21         { total[who] = points[ACELOW]; }  /* Keeps all Aces
                                                     as 1 */
        else
21         { total[who] = points[ACEHIGH]; }  /* Keeps all Aces
                                                     as 11 */

11      if (who == PLAYER)  /* Determines the message printed */
4          { printf("You have a total of %d\n\n", total[PLAYER]); }
        else
           { printf("The house stands with a total of %d\n\n",
4                   total[DEALER]); }
30      return;
     }


3    /**************************************************************
        Prints the winning player.  */
28   void findWinner(int total[2])
     {
```

```
11      if (total[DEALER] == 21)
 4        { printf("The house wins.\n");
30          return;}
12      if ((total[DEALER] > 21) && (total[PLAYER] > 21))
 4        { printf("%s", "Nobody wins.\n");
30          return; }
12      if ((total[DEALER]>=total[PLAYER])&&(total[DEALER]<21))
 4        { printf("The house wins.\n");
30          return; }
12      if ((total[PLAYER] > 21) && (total[DEALER] < 21))
 4        { printf("The house wins.\n");
30          return; }
 4      printf("%s%c", "You win!\n", BELL);
30      return;
      }


 3  /*************************************************************
      Gets the user's uppercase, single-character response. */
28  char getAns(char mesg[])
      {
 5      char ans;
 4      printf("%s", mesg);   /* Prints the prompt message passed */
18      ans = getchar();
        getchar();   /* Discards newline. You can safely */
                     /* ignore compiler warning here.    */
19      return toupper(ans);
      }


 3  /*************************************************************
      Clears everything off the screen. */
28  void dispTitle(void)
      {
 5      int i = 0;
14      while (i < 25)      /* Clears screen by printing 25 blank */
 4        { printf("\n");   /* lines to "push off" stuff that      */
13          i++; }          /* might be left over on the screen    */
                            /* before this program                 */
 4      printf("\n\n*Step right up to the Blackjack tables*\n\n");
30      return;
      }
```

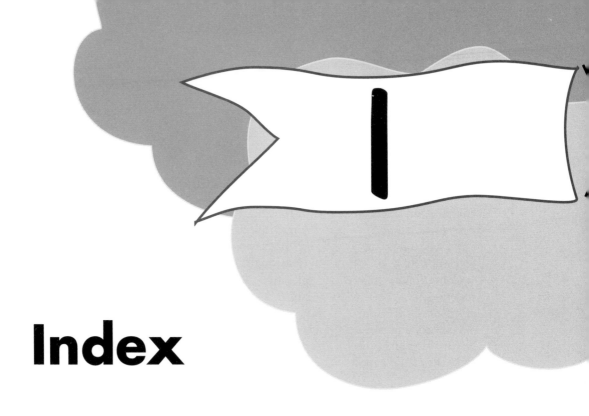

Index

Add to Your Sams Library Today with the Best Books for Programming, Operating Systems, and New Technologies

The easiest way to order is to pick up the phone and call

1-800-428-5331

between 9:00 a.m. and 5:00 p.m. EST.
For faster service please have your credit card available.

ISBN	Quantity	Description of Item	Unit Cost	Total Cost
0-672-30040-0		Teach Yourself C in 21 Days	$24.95	
0-672-30168-7		Advanced C (book/disk)	$39.95	
0-672-30080-X		Moving from C to C++	$29.95	
0-672-30200-4		C++ Programming 101 (book/disk)	$29.95	
0-672-30280-2		Turbo C++ Programming 101 (book/disk)	$29.95	
0-672-30158-X		Advanced C++ (book/disk)	$39.95	
0-672-22687-1		The Waite Group's New C Primer Plus	$29.95	
0-672-48518-4		C Programming for UNIX	$29.95	
0-672-30229-2		Turbo C++ for Windows Programming for Beginners (book/disk)	$39.95	
0-672-30326-4		Absolute Beginner's Guide to Networking	$19.95	
0-672-30282-9		Absolute Beginner's Guide to Memory Management	$16.95	
0-672-30248-9		FractalVision (book/disk)	$39.95	
0-672-30249-7		Multimedia Madness! (book/disk/CD-ROM)	$44.95	
0-672-30310-8		Windows Graphics FunPack (book/disk)	$19.95	
0-672-30318-3		Windows Sound FunPack (book/disk)	$19.95	
0-672-30309-4		Prog. Sound for DOS and Windows (book/disk)	$39.95	
❏ 3 ½" Disk		Shipping and Handling: See information below.		
❏ 5 ¼" Disk		TOTAL		

Shipping and Handling: $4.00 for the first book, and $1.75 for each additional book. Floppy disk: add $1.75 for shipping and handling. If you need to have it NOW, we can ship the product to you in 24 hours for an additional charge of approximately $18.00, and you will receive your item overnight or in two days. Overseas shipping and handling adds $2.00 per book and $8.00 for up to three disks. Prices subject to change. Call for availability and pricing information on latest editions.

11711 N. College Avenue, Suite 140, Carmel, Indiana 46032

1-800-428-5331 — Orders   1-800-835-3202 — FAX   1-800-858-7674 — Customer Service

Book ISBN 0-672-30341-8